PEYTON MANNING

PEYTON MANNING

A QUARTERBACK FOR THE AGES

JIM SACCOMANO AND CRAIG KELLEY
FOREWORD BY TONY DUNGY

SPORTS
PUBLISHING

Sports Publishing books may be purchased in bulk at special discounts for sales promotion, corporate gifts, fund-raising, or educational purposes. Special editions can also be created to specifications. For details, contact the Special Sales Department, Sports Publishing, 307 West 36th Street, 11th Floor, New York, NY 10018 or sportspubbooks@skyhorsepublishing.com.

Sports Publishing® is a registered trademark of Skyhorse Publishing, Inc.®, a Delaware corporation.

 Visit our website at www.sportspubbooks.com.

10 9 8 7 6 5 4 3 2 1

Library of Congress Cataloging-in-Publication Data is available on file.

Cover design by Tom Lau

Cover photo credits: Associated Press

ISBN: 978-1-61321-976-8

Ebook ISBN: 978-1-61321-979-9

Printed in China

To my family, who are always there for me and who love the Broncos as much as I do—my wife JoAnn, my children Jennifer and Jeff, and to the inspiration for this book, my grandchildren and special angels, Lucas and Rhea.

—Jim Saccomano

To my late mother, Louise, and my dear wife, Katie—the women who respectively shaped and shared my most special football memories. Mom's favorite player was Archie Manning and Katie loved Peyton's dedication to excellence.

—Craig Kelley

CONTENTS

Foreword

TONY DUNGY

I met Peyton Manning for the first time at the Maxwell Awards Banquet in February of 1998. I had just finished my second year of coaching the Tampa Bay Buccaneers and Peyton was being honored as the College Football Player of the Year. Immediately, you detected something special with him. On top of the physical skills that were so obvious throughout his college career, I saw an intelligent, engaging young man with natural leadership skills. Spending some time with him that night, it wasn't hard to see he would have a bright future in the NFL.

I had no idea, however, just how brightly his star would shine over the next eighteen years in the National Football League. And I certainly didn't know that I would have the privilege of being his coach for seven of those years. It was a blessing from God for me, not only to be able to coach him but to get to know him as a person.

Our Colts teams won a lot of games during those seven years, including Super Bowl XLI against the Chicago Bears. But to me, the true greatness of Peyton Manning is not found in the Super Bowl rings, MVP trophies, or passing records. As great as those accomplishments are, I always was more impressed with how Peyton accepted the challenge of being a leader off the field as well. His commitment to preparation, to helping his teammates, and to impacting the communities where he lived was what set him apart from others.

In *Peyton Manning: A Quarterback for the Ages*, Craig Kelley and Jim Saccomano, two men who have seen his professional career from a unique point of view, have captured the essence of Peyton

Manning, both on and off the field. They have chronicled his journey in an amazing collection of photographs with behind the scenes stories and anecdotes that bring the photos to life. If a picture is worth a thousand words this book will tell you millions of stories. It will be priceless to anyone who is a fan of Peyton Manning, the NFL, or who simply appreciates a talented athlete who was totally dedicated to making his teams and his community better.

Introduction

From his birth in New Orleans through his time at the Isidore Newman School in the Crescent City, at the University of Tennessee, then with the Indianapolis Colts and the Denver Broncos, Manning truly checked every box of greatness along the way.

When the reality of career accomplishment exceeds all hyperbole, that is most remarkable indeed. Such is the stuff of his career and influence.

The NFL's career leader in combined regular season and postseason wins (200) by a starting quarterback, Manning is the only quarterback in league history to lead two teams to a Super Bowl victory. He quarterbacked the Denver Broncos to a win in Super Bowl 50 to end the 2015 season and his incredible career, after earning his first World Championship with the Indianapolis Colts in Super Bowl XLI following the 2006 season.

Manning is the only five-time Most Valuable Player in NFL history. No player in league history has earned more Pro Bowl appearances (14) than Manning, a fourteen-time team captain who finished his career as the NFL's all-time record holder in career touchdown passes (539) and passing yards (71,940).

Selected by the Colts with the number one overall pick in the 1998 NFL Draft after his brilliant career at Tennessee, Manning started the first 208 games of his career, which set the NFL record for any position.

Manning earned eleven Pro Bowl selections in fourteen years in Indianapolis while being named to the NFL's All-Decade Team for the 2000s. He was named NFL MVP four times (2003 and 2004,

2008 and 2009) as a Colt and led the team to eleven playoff appearances, including nine consecutive postseason berths and 10-plus win seasons from 2002 to 2010. He also helped Indianapolis set the NFL record for the most consecutive seasons with at least 12 victories (seven, 2003-09).

Manning joined the Broncos as a free agent on March 20, 2012, after those fourteen glorious years in Indianapolis.

During his four years in Denver Manning helped the Broncos to the most wins (55) and highest winning percentage (.764) of any team in the NFL while becoming the first quarterback in team history to be a part of four consecutive AFC West titles. No player threw more touchdowns (151) in the regular season/playoffs combined from 2012-15 than Manning, who ranked third in the league in overall passer rating (99.6) as well as fourth in both overall passing yards (19,062) and completions (1,639).

In 2013 Manning posted the most prolific season of any quarterback in NFL history en route to earning his fifth MVP award and receiving *Sports Illustrated's* prestigious Sportsman of the Year award. Manning, who led the Broncos to their first Super Bowl appearance in fifteen years, set the all-time NFL single-season records for touchdown passes (55) and passing yards (5,477) while leading the highest scoring offense (606 points, 37.9 per game) in NFL history.

And all of those Denver accomplishments came after many thought his career was over.

Manning's first season with the Broncos in 2012 saw him earn the Associated Press Comeback Player of the Year award for his remarkable return to the field from a neck injury and four subsequent surgeries that forced him to miss the 2011 season. He went on to set Bronco single-season records in every major passing category and finished second in the MVP voting that year.

During his superlative regular-season career Manning played 266 games (265 starts and a 186-79 record) and completed 6,125 passes for 71,940 yards with 539 touchdowns. For good measure, he added 667 yards and 18 touchdowns rushing.

Leading his teams to an NFL-record fifteen playoff appearances, Manning had 43 touchdowns, 40 passing and three rushing, and took four of his eighteen playoff teams to Super Bowl berths.

In addition to his on-field contributions, his community work is a litany of giving. Manning has been involved actively in the community throughout his playing career. His PeyBack Foundation, which was established in 1999 to promote the future success of disadvantaged youth, has provided more than $11 million of positive impact in the states of Louisiana, Tennessee, Indiana, and Colorado.

The recipient of numerous local and national recognitions for his community involvement, Manning is one of only eight players in NFL history to win all three of the league's most prestigious community awards—the Byron "Whizzer" White Humanitarian Award (2004), the Walter Payton NFL Man of the Year Award (2005), and the Bart Starr Award (2015).

Manning continues to be involved with St. Vincent's Children's Hospital in Indianapolis, which in 2007 was renamed the Peyton Manning Children's Hospital at St. Vincent's. At the University of Tennessee, his alma mater, he created the Peyton Manning Scholarship Program that has provided for 25 incoming students in the last eighteen years on the basis of academic achievement, leadership and community service.

In words and pictures, with comments from many others, this book is a walk down the path of Peyton Manning's football journey.

PEYTON MANNING

QUARTER 1

A LEGEND IN THE MAKING

Peyton Manning is the middle of three sons of Olivia and Archie Manning. Peyton was raised with integrity in sport and life, played high school football with his brother, and ultimately graduated in three years from the University of Tennessee.

A framed jersey and photos of the Manning brothers sit in an office in Isidore Newman School in New Orleans.

It All Began in New Orleans

An All-American quarterback at the University of Mississippi (Ole Miss), Archie Manning was selected as the second overall pick in the 1971 NFL Draft by the New Orleans Saints. He played for eleven seasons in New Orleans, one season for the Houston Oilers, and finished his career in 1984 with the Minnesota Vikings.

The family stayed in New Orleans after Archie's retirement and Peyton and his brothers attended the Isidore Newman School. The 1991 Newman season was special for the Manning family. It was the only one in which Peyton and his brother Cooper played on the same team. "I doubt I could adequately explain how much fun that year was," said Peyton in the 2000 book, *Manning*. "I can tell you it was the *most* fun I ever had playing football. For me football was always fun, from the games on the rug (with Cooper and Archie years earlier) to the games in the yard to the "Amazing Catches" to the videotaping to the Christmas uniforms, and even to right now, when I'm playing at the top level and still having fun. But 1991 was like no other."

During high school games, Peyton and Cooper used coded communications to play pitch-and-catch, as Manning later would do with wide receiver Marvin Harrison in Indianapolis. He estimated that half of his 200 attempts in 1991 were directed toward Cooper as Newman reached the state semifinals.

"The way he looks, the way he throws, I would have thought Peyton was a junior in college, not in high school." — Jim Mora, who let Manning participate in Saints off-season practices

The future turned bright orange at the University of Tennessee, where a young Manning led the Volunteers to a Southeastern Conference Championship as a senior in 1997 and finished as a consensus All-American.

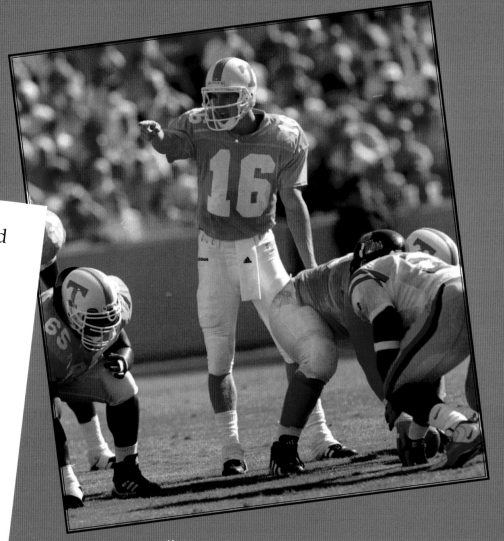

"What Peyton was able to accomplish reminded me of what Larry Bird did his in senior year at Indiana State. He personally played the role of taking his team where it went."
—Indianapolis Colts president Bill Polian

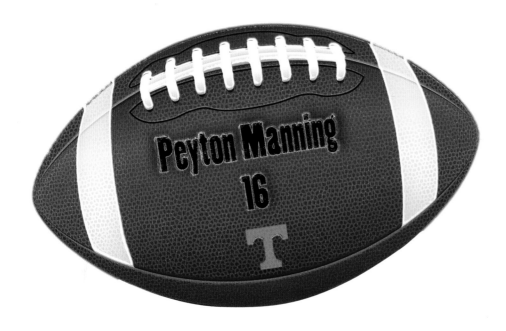

"I cherished my time in Knoxville, especially my senior year. And I want Vols fans everywhere to know the unique role that you've played in my life."

—Peyton Manning

Peyton Manning's College Stats								
Year	GP	Att.	Cmp.	Pct.	Yards	Int.	TDs	Team's Record
1994– Freshman	10	144	89	61.8	1,141	6	11	8 – 4
1995– Sophomore	12	380	244	64.2	2,954	4	22	11 – 1
1996– Junior	13	380	243	63.9	3,287	12	20	10 – 2
1997– Senior	13	477	287	60.2	3,819	11	36	11 – 2
Career Total:	48	1381	863	62.5	11,201	33	89	40 – 9

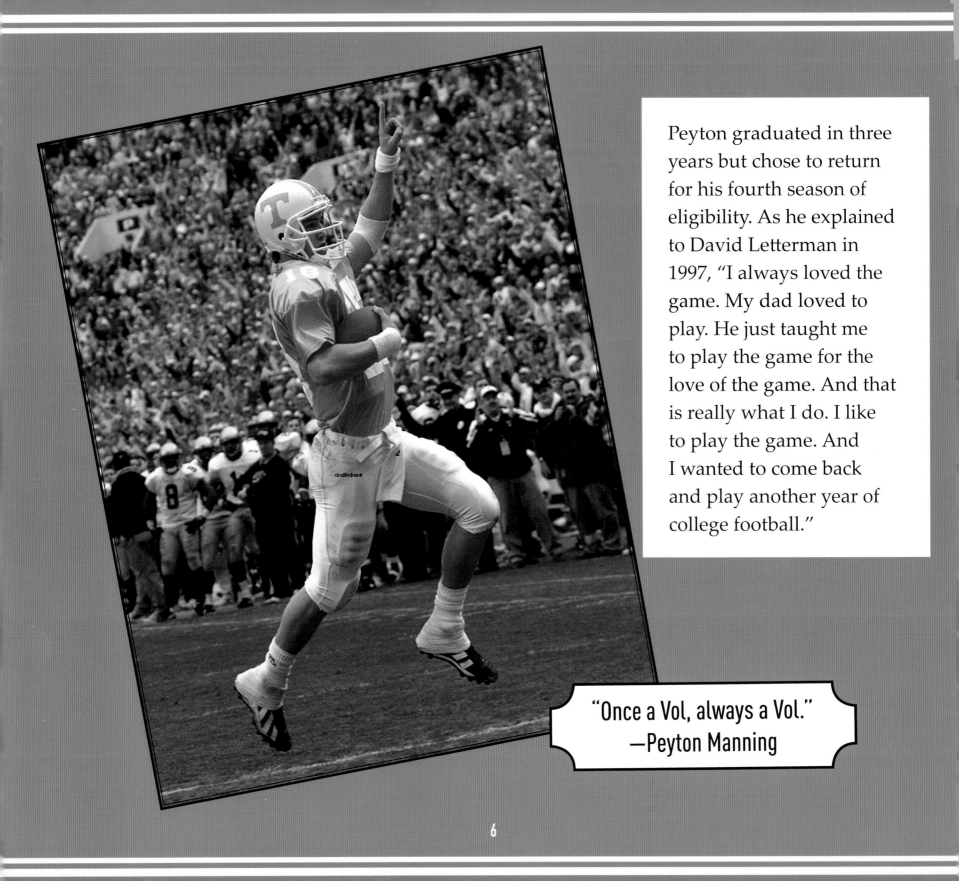

Peyton graduated in three years but chose to return for his fourth season of eligibility. As he explained to David Letterman in 1997, "I always loved the game. My dad loved to play. He just taught me to play the game for the love of the game. And that is really what I do. I like to play the game. And I wanted to come back and play another year of college football."

"Once a Vol, always a Vol."
—Peyton Manning

QUARTER 2

A RHAPSODY IN BLUE

Peyton Manning joined one of the most revered franchises in sports and returned the Colts to prominence with his excellence—once again returning the iconic "horseshoe" to the gallery of champions.

The First Pick in the Draft

Colts owner Jim Irsay, left, and NFL Commissioner Paul Tagliabue, flank the top pick in the 1998 NFL Draft.

After being the face of Tennessee football, Manning practically inherited the same role upon joining the Colts as the first overall pick in the 1998 NFL Draft.

Colts president Bill Polian and head coach Jim Mora ultimately decided on Manning as their first pick. It proved to be a fateful decision. The franchise, which was steeped in quarterbacking lore, had started sixteen different signal-callers between 1983 and 1997, and that changed when number 18 arrived on the scene.

Peyton Manning's First Audible

As Jim Irsay's plane carrying the Manning family and a small Colts contingent approached Indianapolis coming from the NFL Draft, the pilot encountered a landing delay from the tower. Manning had done two hours of interviews in New York and had 10 more to conduct in a tight 45-minute window. He was flying to Knoxville that night to be honored, so time was critical. The snap decision was made to put Manning on the headset to ask for clearance. The controller heard Manning's request, cleared traffic and ordered the plane to land immediately. Manning had audibled into his first Colts touchdown. Here, Peyton and Archie Manning arrive at the Colts' headquarters on April 18, 1998.

"Listen, I just want to leave you with this one thought: if you draft me, I promise we will win a championship."
—Peyton Manning to Colts GM Bill Polian ahead of the 1998 Draft

"I can't say that I envisioned everything that Peyton Manning would become, but after you have been through this process, which you trust, everything pointed to him."
—Bill Polian

Why 18?

Manning originally wanted to wear number 18 at Tennessee to honor his father, Archie, but it was unavailable. He sought number 12 for former UT quarterback Bobby Scott, who backed up Archie many years in New Orleans. It, too, was unavailable, so Manning chose number 16. Knowing the first pick in the draft would be either Manning or Ryan Leaf (who also wore number 16 at Washington State), the Colts planned to order a large quantity of number 16 jerseys to be ready for the demands the organization would face. When Manning informed the Colts he would like number 18 if he were chosen so he could honor his father, a club official told Bill Polian backup wide receiver Nate Jacquet wore 18. Replied Polian, "Not anymore!"

Manning's Rookie Season

"The sooner you take your lumps, the better off you're going to be in the long run. . . . Experience is your best teacher."
—Peyton Manning, on being named the starter in 1998

In 1998, Manning started 16 games, the first of 13 straight seasons doing so with Indianapolis. He set NFL rookie records in completions (326), attempts (575), yards (3,739), touchdowns (26), 300-yard games (4), 3-TD games (4) and consecutive games with a TD pass (13) and took every snap from scrimmage. Manning was the seventh-youngest opening-day rookie starter in history, just behind his father, Archie, the sixth-youngest.

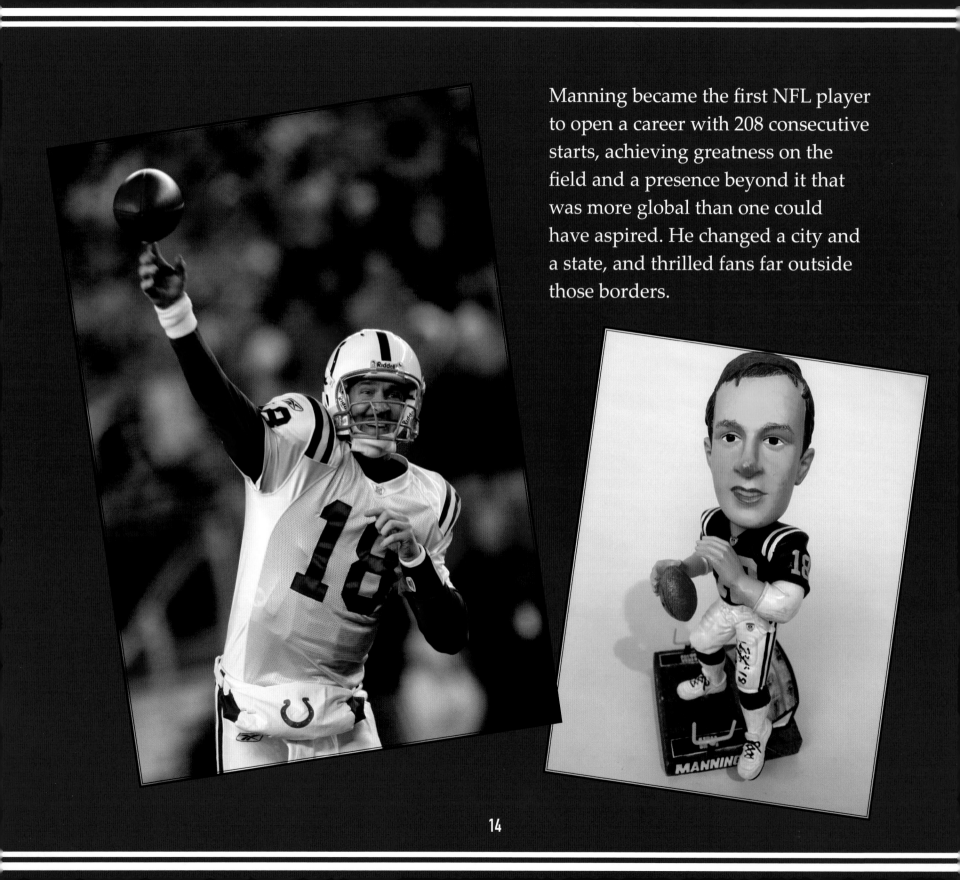

Manning became the first NFL player to open a career with 208 consecutive starts, achieving greatness on the field and a presence beyond it that was more global than one could have aspired. He changed a city and a state, and thrilled fans far outside those borders.

A Rookie Milestone

"I've never been big on individual records, but the fact that record was held so long by Charlie Conerly, that's a special thing. I'd still trade it all for some more wins this season, but it's a nice honor."
—Peyton Manning, after he broke the 50-year-old record for touchdown passes by a rookie

"I'm old school. I still believe Johnny Unitas was the game's greatest quarterback because in addition to his physical tools, he called his own plays. He could beat you with his arm, his mind or both. A quarterback calling his own plays is a lost art in the NFL today. That's what I've always liked about Manning. He's the one quarterback today who wouldn't need to look to the sideline for the play call. He could call his own game. We've all seen him do it. Peyton Manning could play in any era because of his command of the huddle, command of the line of scrimmage, command of his playbook and command of the opposing defense. And he'd be a great quarterback in any era."
—Pro Football HOF voter Rick Gosselin

"You're not going to fool Peyton Manning. He knows where he's going with the football before the snap."
—Brian Urlacher

Perfecting every aspect of his game meant extensive work at ball fakes, a Manning specialty that put him among the best. Legendary Colts coach Ted Marchibroda (pictured in the background), who knew John Unitas as a rookie and worked with other great NFL QBs in prior eras, marveled at Manning's detailed work and said Manning measured up against history's finest players.

Peyton Manning and center Jeff Saturday started 170 games together, the record for most games started by a quarterback-center combination.

"I'll always be indebted to what Jeff has done for me, just protecting me as a quarterback."
—Peyton Manning

"To see those two guys work together is a work of art."
—Jim Caldwell

"We used to call him 'Coach Manning' and used to bust him up about how hard he worked. He showed up early. He left late. He led by example. He never expected you to give anything that he wasn't going to give himself."
—Jeff Saturday

Manning-Dungy: A Winning Combination

After coaching Tampa Bay from 1996 to 2001, Tony Dungy became head coach of the Indianapolis Colts in 2002. Over the next seven seasons, Peyton Manning and Dungy became one of history's winningest quarterback-head coach combinations, compiling an 85-27 mark and a World Championship. They never won fewer than ten games in a season or missed the playoffs. Manning helped Dungy become the first coach to beat all thirty-two teams, while Manning beat every opponent as a Colt.

"He's probably the hardest-working guy I've been around who has great ability. Overachievers work hard because they have to. Peyton has rare talent, but chooses to push himself like he doesn't. I've never seen a guy with so much ability and the dedication to match."
—Tony Dungy

Manning had an 85-27 starting record under Tony Dungy, the most wins by a starting QB under a head coach in Colts history (55-20-3, John Unitas-Don Shula; 49-33, Unitas-Weeb Ewbank). Said Dungy, "He was special in wanting to prepare and wanting to win and wanting to be coached." Manning's 54 game-winning drives in the fourth quarter or overtime are the most in the 1970 post-Merger era, and one Houdini escape in 2003 at Tampa Bay (down 35-14 with four minutes left to a 38-35 OT win) left commentator John Madden aghast: "It was totally beyond belief. I've never seen or taken part in a comeback like that in my life." Manning and Dungy are shown here celebrating the win.

"Peyton is a great quarterback. Anybody who doesn't know that, doesn't know much about football."
—Tony Dungy

An MVP Season

"Obviously you look at all the former winners, it really is an honor to be on that same list, and to have such great teammates and a coaching staff that allowed me to go out and make plays. And to be sharing it with Steve, a player I have the most respect for and who has had a tremendous year, and to be ahead of guys like Tom Brady, who's a friend of mine, and Jamal Lewis, a former teammate of mine at Tennessee who easily could have been there, as well, it's tremendous."
—Peyton Manning

In 2003, Manning set the club passing percentage record (67.0) and had 20+ completions and 200+ yards in 14 games. The club's 5-0 start included erasing a 21-point deficit at Tampa Bay with four minutes left on the way to an overtime win, the first NFL team to accomplish the feat. He surpassed John Unitas' positional record of 92 starts on December 7 at Tennessee and had his first six-TD effort at New Orleans on September 28. Manning led club to the AFC Championship game and won first of five NFL MVP awards. He was a co-MVP with the Tennessee Titans' Steve McNair.

A Dynamic Duo

Wide receiver Marvin Harrison arrived in Indianapolis two years before Manning and saw the future immediately. "When Peyton got here, I saw a quarterback who works as hard as I do. … I thought, 'This could be something.'"

What it turned out to be was one of the greatest quarterback-receiver combinations in NFL history. Peyton Manning and Marvin Harrison set records for a duo that are likely to stand forever: 953 completions, 12,766 yards, and 112 touchdowns.

October 17, 2005: Manning and Harrison after the 86th of their 112 touchdown connections. They broke the record held by Steve Young and Jerry Rice.

"The very first preseason game, my very first pass, I threw a five-yard pass, and Marvin Harrison ran 48 yards for a touchdown. I remember thinking, 'The NFL is easy. You just throw a short pass and Marvin Harrison will run for touchdowns.' Which is pretty much what he did for the entire time we played together. I think many records will be broken—most of my records will be broken—I don't believe that record that me and Marvin have of throwing the most touchdowns together will ever be broken." —Peyton Manning

"We both see the same thing. I think that's what makes Peyton and me that much better together. We both see the same thing before it happens." —Marvin Harrison

Manning-to-Harrison—they did it their way!

Repeat MVP

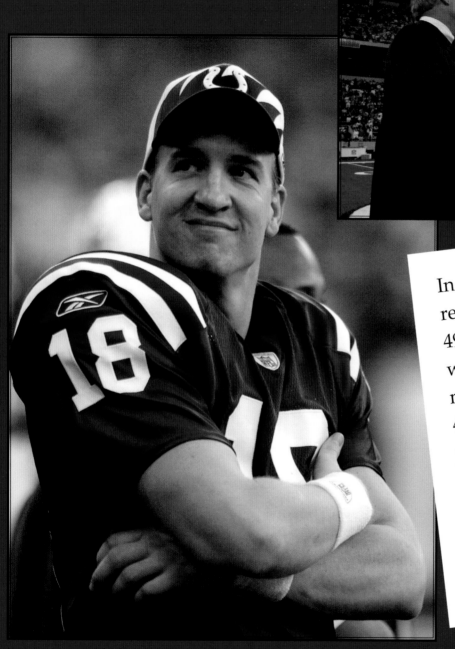

In 2004, Manning was the repeat NFL MVP recipient who set the NFL seasonal record of 49 touchdown passes. He set an NFL mark with a 121.1 passer rating and reset franchise marks with a 67.7 completion percentage and 4,557 yards. Manning became the only NFL player with 10+ touchdown passes to three different receivers. He had 4+ TD passes in six games and tortured NFC foes with 19 touchdown passes and a 4-0 record. He threw for 458 yards and four TDs in a playoff win over Denver.

All-Pro Trio

Marvin Harrison, Peyton Manning, and Edgerrin James on February 12, 2006. They were Pro Bowl starters and appeared together for the last time as "The Triplets." With Manning, Harrison and James each topped 100 yards in the same game an NFL-record 22 times.

Peyton Manning, Edgerrin James, and Marvin Harrison in the tunnel prior to a 2005 game against Houston.

Peyton Manning talks with Colts offensive coodinator Tom Moore on the sidelines in Indianapolis, Sunday, January 1, 2006.

"I think the Lord taught him that."
—Tom Moore on Manning's fabled ability to make changes at the line of scrimmage.

"He called the touchdowns. I called the interceptions."
—Tom Moore

In 2005, Manning helped trigger a 13-0 start with 3,747 passing yards and 28 touchdowns. He was a first-team All-Pro for the third straight year and the Colts set a franchise record with 14 victories.

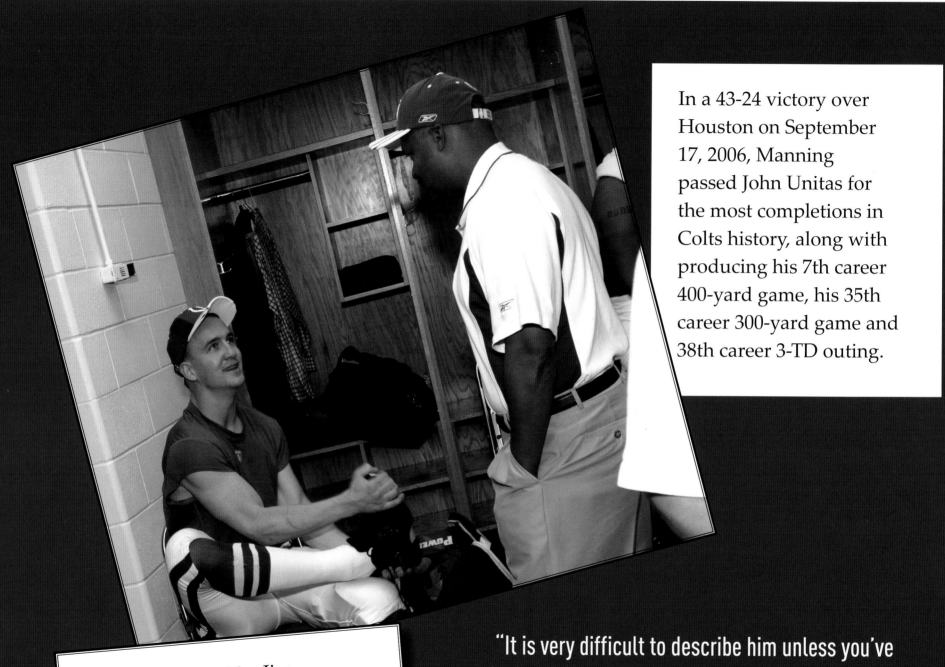

In a 43-24 victory over Houston on September 17, 2006, Manning passed John Unitas for the most completions in Colts history, along with producing his 7th career 400-yard game, his 35th career 300-yard game and 38th career 3-TD outing.

Getting debriefed by Jim Caldwell after another wondrous performance.

"It is very difficult to describe him unless you've worked with him. He is absolutely phenomenal. Just an unbelievable recall that's just entirely extraordinary. That's what sets him apart." — Jim Caldwell

On January 21, 2007, the Colts erased an 18-point deficit with a 32-point second half in a 38-34 AFC Championship game win over New England. Manning threw for 349 yards and had one-yard TD rush as the club had second-half scoring drives of 76, 76, 67, 59 and 80 yards, the last ending with 1:00 left. The Colts reached the Super Bowl for the first time since the 1970 season.

Manning on the game-winning drive against New England in the 2007 AFC Championship game. Down 21-3, Manning and his mates rebounded for a 38-34 win. In Manning fashion, the Colts drove 80 yards for a TD in the waning seconds.

A World Championship

Peyton Manning lived up to a pre-draft promise by making the Colts winners. Manning elevated Indianapolis among the NFL's elite franchises and returned the Colts to the championship circle with a 29-17 victory over Chicago in Super Bowl XLI.

Already revolutionizing how his position was played, Manning took his place in the gallery of champions in the first of four eventual Super Bowl appearances.

A rainy night in Miami warmed the hearts of Colts fans as Manning guided the franchise to its first World Championship in 31 years, winning MVP honors.

"In the past when our teams come up short, it's been disappointing," Manning said. "It's nice when you put a lot of hard work to cap it off with a championship."

Becoming the third person to win a Super Bowl as a player and head coach, Tony Dungy already knew Manning's stature, "If people think he needed to win a Super Bowl, that is wrong. This guy is a Hall of Fame player and one of the greatest ever."

Peyton Manning and the Colts move the chains for a first down during their 29-17 victory over the Chicago Bears in Super Bowl XLI. Manning was the game's MVP.

"It was a wonderful team game. Everyone did their job" —Peyton Manning

Manning-Brady

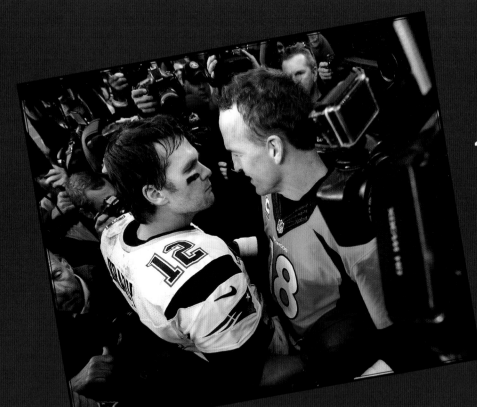

"Peyton Manning is the best quarterback I've ever coached against. He does it all. He makes all the throws, great at the line of scrimmage, does a great job reading defenses, puts his players and teammates in good positions to make plays—big plays in critical situations."
—Bill Belichick

Every football fan knows that quarterbacks aren't on the field at the same time, so they don't face each other. Teams play each other. But quarterback rivalries have been the stuff of hot stove debates for generations. Unitas vs. Starr. Namath vs. Lamonica. Staubach vs. Bradshaw. Montana vs. Aikman. Elway vs. Kosar. Marino vs. Kelly.

Peyton Manning and the New England Patriots' quarterback Tom Brady faced each other seventeen times over the course of fifteen seasons. Whether the game was an early-season matchup or the AFC championship, each QB often brought out the best in his counterpart. Manning and Brady faced off four times in a championship game—the most in the Super Bowl era.

"Who has lived up to the expectations year after year after year as well as Peyton? He's done it so gracefully, so admirably. He set the standard for how to play the quarterback position."
—Tom Brady

"I know Manning is definitely worthy of the award. He's an outstanding player and I take my hat off to him."
—Adrian Peterson

Despite having knee surgery prior to the season and missing all of the preseason, Manning earned his third NFL MVP Award in 2008, tying Brett Favre, John Unitas, and Jim Brown for the most in history. During the season, he had his 32nd of 45 fourth-quarter comebacks/OT game-winning drives to surpass the club mark set by John Unitas. He became the only NFL quarterback with 10+ starting wins in seven straight seasons. Indianapolis extended its NFL-record streak to six straight seasons with 12+ wins by sweeping its last nine games.

2009: Another MVP Season

In 2009, Manning led the Colts to a 14-0 start, the conference title and to Super Bowl XLIV, winning an unprecedented fourth NFL MVP. The Colts were comeback kings with four straight last-quarter triumphs in November. The 14-0 start gave Indianapolis a league-record 23 consecutive wins. He had 393 completions, 4,500 yards and 33 TDs, and Manning's 119th starting win at Miami on September 21 broke the club mark of John Unitas. His 68.8 completion percentage marked a career-best.

On November 15, 2009, the Colts overcame two 17-point deficits, one in the last quarter, for a 35-34 win over New England. Manning (28-44-327, 4 TDs) led three fourth-quarter TD drives, two in the final four minutes. An 18th straight win let the Colts become the only team with three 9-0 starts in a five-year span.

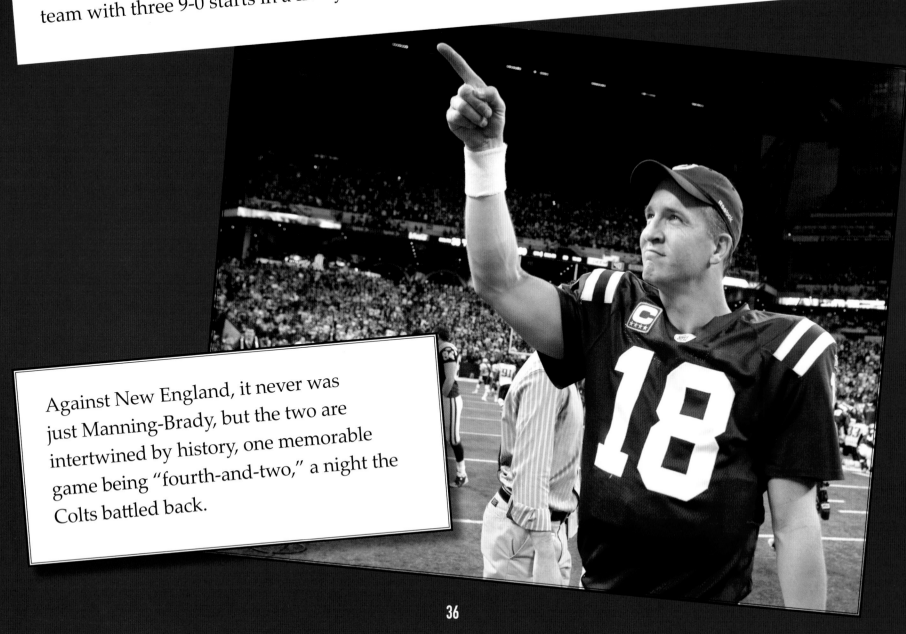

Against New England, it never was just Manning-Brady, but the two are intertwined by history, one memorable game being "fourth-and-two," a night the Colts battled back.

On December 17, 2009, in a 35-31 win at Jacksonville, the Colts earned two NFL records—their 23rd straight win and their 115th regular season win of the decade (2000-09). Tying a franchise record with 14 victories and amassing 11 straight road wins, Manning led the Colts to playoff wins against Baltimore and the Jets in reaching Super Bowl XLIV.

The juggernaut Colts played for all the marbles twice during Manning's fabled command.

All in the Family

Peyton and Eli Manning were taken with the first overall pick in their respective NFL drafts—1998 and 2004—while Archie was the second overall choice in 1971.

"We tried to raise kids, not quarterbacks."
—Archie Manning

Peyton and Eli first met on the football in the 2006 opener, "I know it's going to be difficult and awkward for my family and my parents, and I know they will just try to get through it."

Peyton's teams eventually won all three meetings against the Giants, adding a difficult emotional element to a very tight-knit family.

"It's a strange feeling. It's not like beating another team. It's not quite as enjoyable as it would be if you were beating somebody else."
—Peyton Manning, after his Broncos defeated brother Eli's Giants, 41-23

"The records and awards don't define his glory or explain his passion."
—Eli Manning, on his brother Peyton

Of the brother and father-son combinations to make the NFL, none have closer bonds than the Mannings. Here, Archie Manning congratulates Peyton in 2004 after he broke Dan Marino's record for touchdowns thrown in a season.

Peyton and Eli Manning during a visit to Isidore Newman School in New Orleans, 2015. The event was part of the Super Bowl 50 High School Honor Roll, in which the NFL commemorated the game with a presentation of a gold football to the high school of each Super Bowl participant of the first five decades. The Manning family is one of NFL royalty. Peyton and Eli have been the winning quarterbacks in four of the last ten Super Bowls.

Rarely Off Broadway

Manning directed the Colts to 48 prime-time appearances, with 33 wins. The Colts had not played in that many prime-time games in franchise history before his arrival. In the photo below, Manning and the Colts warm up prior to a game against the Giants in 2010.

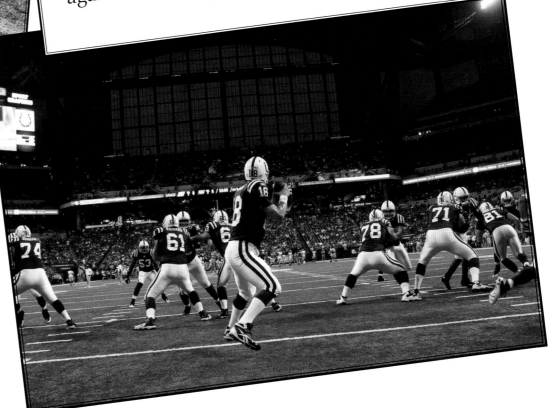

Manning's late 27-yard run and slide milked the final seconds off the clock in gritty win against the Oakland Raiders at the Black Hole, on December 26, 2010. Manning's 207th game played broke the club mark of John Unitas and put the Colts in the playoffs for the ninth straight year.

In 2010, Manning led the Colts to a ninth straight post-season with a 10-6 record. He had an NFL-record 11th 4,000-yard passing season and a league-best 13th straight year with 25+ touchdowns and 3,000 yards. A wild card defeat marked Manning's last game as a Colt.

Number 18 always will be Number One in the hearts of Colts fans. The ways in which he transformed a city, state, and franchise are incalculable.

QUARTER 3

SUNSET IN ORANGE AND BLUE

In 2012, Peyton Manning joined the Denver Broncos and added to his own and the team's brilliant history of records and championships.

Peyton Manning had quarterbacked the Indianapolis Colts every Sunday since September 6, 1998. On September 11, 2011, while recovering from neck surgery, he watched from the sidelines as the Colts took on the Houston Texans in their season opener. He would miss the entire 2011 season due to injury and became an unrestricted free agent the following year.

He joined the Denver Broncos as a free agent in March 2012, in a signing that ranks as one of the two greatest player acquisitions in Broncos history—the other being the trade that brought John Elway to Denver in 1983. Manning, center, is flanked by Broncos owner Pat Bowlin, left, and vice president John Elway during a news conference at the NFL Denver Broncos headquarters on March 20, 2012.

"Peyton Manning raises all boats."
—John Elway, on the occasion of Peyton Manning's signing with Denver

During an August 12, 2012 preseason game against the Seahawks, Broncos fans show their support of the Broncos' new quarterback.

Peyton Manning signs autographs during training camp in August 2013.

"It's quite an honor for me to wear number 18 for the Denver Broncos. I spoke to Frank Tripucka [the Broncos' first quarterback], and I spoke with his wife, and they were telling me they wanted me to wear number 18. . . . After his passing, we had a great visit with the Tripucka family. That was a special moment for me."
—Peyton Manning

"I would be honored to have Peyton Manning wear [number 18]. It's been retired for 50 years! That's long enough!"
—Frank Tripucka

Peyton Manning during an August 2012 preseason game. Manning was chosen as the NFL Comeback Player of the Year by the Associated Press in 2012 and finished second in MVP voting following his first season with the Broncos. He would lead the Broncos to the AFC West title in each of his four years. Further tribute to his brilliance is that Peyton Manning is the only player in history to be named NFL Most Valuable Player five times (2003-04, 2008-09, 2013). The next highest NFL total is three.

"To come back after the injury he had. . .it takes a special guy. To come to a new team, new teammates, new city—everything about it new other than the conference—it's pretty amazing, actually." —former Broncos head coach John Fox

"Peyton Manning revolutionized the game. We used to think a no-huddle was fast pace, and we would try to figure out the coverage on the way back to the pocket. But he basically said, 'I'm going to find out what you're doing and then I'm going to pick you apart.' I can't tell you how many times I looked at it and thought, 'Dang, why didn't we think of that?' But Peyton did think about that, and he changed the game."
—John Elway

"Peyton was a game-changer and opened the door to the passing game that helped the league thrive. Were it not for Peyton Manning, his no-huddle offense and his play out of the shotgun, the NFL might be more of a running league than a passing league."
—John Clayton, ESPN senior writer; member of writers' wing of the Pro Football Hall of Fame

"That's the great thing about Peyton. He makes everyone around him smarter."
—Demaryius Thomas

"My dad told us up front, 'Guys, if you want to play sports, go ahead, but it's your decision.'" —Peyton Manning, quoting advice from his father, Archie.

MANNING IN HIS OWN WORDS

Peyton Manning when asked what he planned to do with the money after signing his rookie contract in 1998: "Earn it."

Peyton Manning on being tough, "My dad told me, 'You've got to be tough.' You hear about reading defenses and all that but if you're not tough, you won't last half a season."

An Unparalled Season

In 2013, Peyton Manning moved past greatness into the stuff of legend with a performance never before seen in professional football.

Just two years after coming to Denver amid serious questions regarding his ability to return from four neck surgeries, and just one year after being named the NFL Comeback Player of the Year—a most remarkable accomplishment for any player of his age—Manning set new standards for future generations by blowing holes in the NFL record book.

It was not even the winning of his oft-referenced fifth NFL MVP award and leading the Broncos to Super Bowl XLVIII, but the astonishing way he did it throughout the year that set the measure for all quarterbacks.

Manning set six new passing records, all of the highest level. He set new marks for passing yards (5,477) and touchdowns (55), 400-yard passing games (four), four-touchdown games (nine), most touchdowns without throwing an interception to start a season (20), and passing first downs (289).

His remarkable performance resulted in Denver having the highest scoring team in NFL history with 606 points.

Those records, taken in total and combined with the record-fifth MVP, give strong credence to the argument that no future quarterback will ever reach all those standards in a single season again.

The *Sports Illustrated* issue honoring Peyton Manning as the magazine's 2013 Sportsman of the Year.

"[Peyton Manning's 2013 season] was just the best year ever of any quarterback."
—Wade Phillips, then the interim coach of the Houston Texans

"I can say I have never seen a better year played by a quarterback than Peyton Manning. To see what he did this year, it was truly amazing."
—John Elway, on Manning's 2013 MVP season

Respect for—and from—Other Greats

Peyton Manning and Brett Favre following a 45-31 Colts win in Indianapolis, Sunday, September 26, 2004.

On October 19, 2014, Peyton Manning passed Brett Favre to set the all-time record with 509 passing touchdowns. Just over a year later, on November 15, 2015, Manning eclipsed Favre's all-time mark of 71,838 passing yards. Manning, Favre, and Dan Marino are the only quarterbacks in league history to have passed for more than 60,000 yards.

"He's very cerebral at the line of scrimmage, calls his own plays, very demanding, a guy that you can tell is in total control of his offense."
—Dan Marino on Peyton Manning

"Congrats for breaking the touchdown record. I'm not surprised. You've been a wonderful player and I've enjoyed watching you play. I've enjoyed competing against you. Again, congratulations."
—Brett Favre

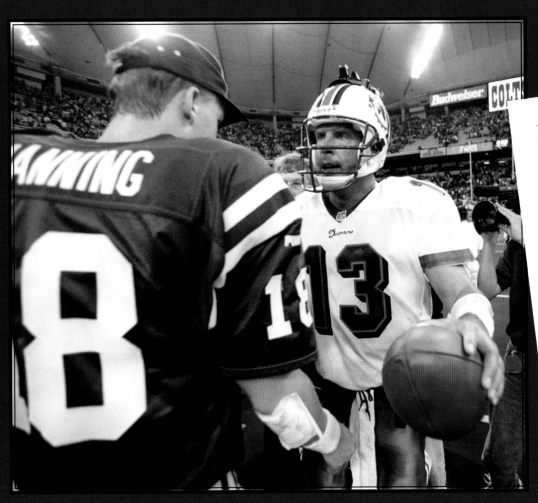

Peyton Manning and Dan Marino following the Dolphins 34-31 win in Indianapolis Sunday, October 10, 1999.

Manning faced Dan Marino in his rookie debut, then broke Marino's single-season touchdown passes mark in 2004. He later took the title back to become the first QB to set the mark twice.

Marvin Harrison scoring on a 39-yard pass from Peyton Manning, September 23, 2001.

These charts illustrate Peyton Manning's top five targets over the course of his career.

Peyton Manning and Reggie Wayne in 2007.

Peyton Manning's Top Five—Touchdown Passes	
Marvin Harrison, Indianapolis Colts	112
Reggie Wayne, Indianapolis Colts	67
Dallas Clark, Indianapolis Colts	44
Demaryius Thomas, Denver Broncos	36
Marcus Pollard, Indianapolis Colts	34

Peyton Manning's Top Five—Reception Yards	
Marvin Harrison, Indianapolis Colts	12,766
Reggie Wayne, Indianapolis Colts	10,602
Demaryius Thomas, Denver Broncos	5,243
Dallas Clark, Indianapolis Colts	4,479
Marcus Pollard, Indianapolis Colts	3,138

Arizona Cardinals head coach Bruce Arians greets Peyton Manning after a preseason football game, Thursday, September 3, 2015, in Denver.

Arians was the Indianapolis Colts' quarterbacks coach during Peyton Manning's first three years with the team.

"His learning curve is amazing. It's like feeding a piranha. He's a piranha of information. ... He eats everything you give him and wants more."
—Bruce Arians

"His competitiveness is off the charts, every day. I can't emphasize enough how much he hates to lose. He hates ever having a practical joke pulled on him that may have been better than the one he pulled on someone else. He loves jabbing people. The fierce competitive nature is there, whether it's football, golf, practical jokes. That competitive spirit drives him. It is to the extreme, and it is non-stop. Peyton does it in a way where he knows he has to perform every day, and it has to be perfect."
—Bruce Arians

"Peyton's encyclopedic memory and ability to process information rapidly often made me think if there were a football version of the movie *A Beautiful Mind*, it would have to be made about him. There are race horses, and then there is Secretariat. Peyton is Secretariat."

—Craig Kelley, former Colts vice president of PR

"Omaha! Omaha!" —Peyton Manning, making arguably the most famous and most repeated audible in NFL history, bringing great pride and enjoyment to residents of that Nebraska city.

"He's going to do what he has to do to win. He's one of the greatest competitors ever in this league."
—Broncos head coach Gary Kubiak

"He has always been a great game manager, but even more so now."
—John Elway

The Broncos and Manning emerged victorious following the AFC Championship game between the Denver Broncos and the New England Patriots, Sunday, January 24, 2016, in Denver. Manning and the Broncos defeated the Patriots 20-18 to advance to the Super Bowl.

Super Bowl 50

Preparation, intense competition, pride and patriotism all came together at Super Bowl 50 in Santa Clara. Above, Peyton Manning watches the flyover just before the greatest victory of his Broncos career.

"Oh wow. Playing the Sheriff. Well either way, we're
going to live in the moment."
—Cam Newton, when he learned that his Carolina
Panthers would be playing the Broncos in Super
Bowl 50

Manning went on to become the first quarterback to win the Super Bowl with two teams and the first to take two franchises to the Super Bowl twice each. He also became the first quarterback to reach the Super Bowl four times with four different head coaches. Manning made his fourth Super Bowl start in Super Bowl 50, third most all-time by any quarterback. He became the oldest quarterback both to start and to win a Super Bowl, at age 39.

In one of the greatest endings of any NFL career, Manning holds the Lombardi Trophy as he is interviewed by Jim Nantz of CBS minutes after Super Bowl 50, Manning's second World Championship and the third for the Denver Broncos. Mrs. Annabel Bowlen is to Peyton's left.

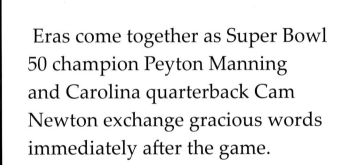

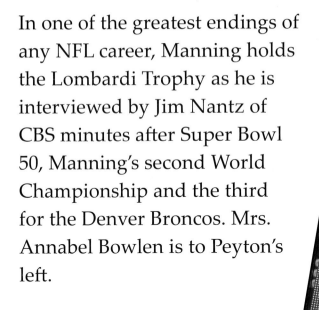

Eras come together as Super Bowl 50 champion Peyton Manning and Carolina quarterback Cam Newton exchange gracious words immediately after the game.

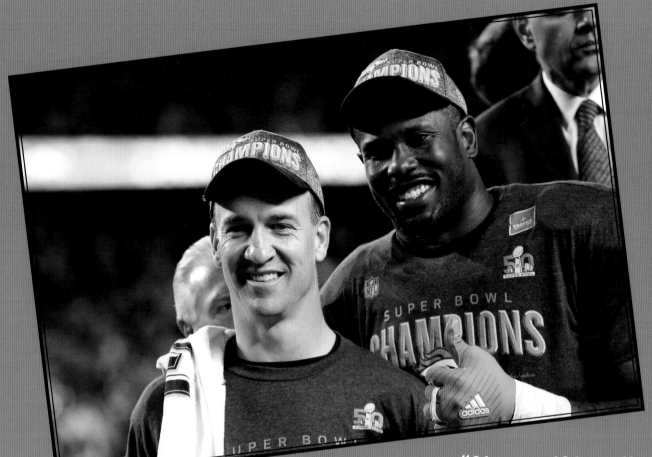

Manning and game MVP Von Miller following the Broncos' 24-10 victory over the Carolina Panthers in Super Bowl 50.

"Of course 18 is my No 1 quarterback. I love everything about him, from the way he handles the media, the way he handles his teammates and his brothers. It's definitely something that I'll take with me for the rest of my life. To watch him lead and to watch him be the leader that everybody knows that he is has definitely been great for me.'
—Von Miller

Return to the Rose Garden

"Rose Garden, Rose Garden!"—using a site-appropriate audible, Manning hits a fan with a pass on the South Lawn of the White House in 2007

On April 23, 2007, the Colts and Peyton Manning were honored by President George W. Bush after winning Super Bowl XLI over Chicago, 29-17. Nine years later, following Super Bowl 50, Manning returned to the Rose Garden with the Broncos at the invitation of President Obama.

Retiring on Top

"I did not get shorted at all in anything football-wise in really my 25 years if you go to high school and college. I got my football fill as a player . . . I have no regrets because I've worked so hard and prepared as hard as I could to get ready to play and so you cannot say that I was shorted. I think I'll be OK."
—Peyton Manning

One month after winning Super Bowl 50 with the Denver Broncos, Peyton Manning held a news conference in Englewood, Colorado, to announce the end of his eighteen-year career as a professional football player. Eight days later, he returned to Indianapolis to say goodbye to the fans who thrilled to his exploits as a Colt.

QUARTER 4

MVP OFF THE FIELD

Peyton Manning wasn't just raised by parents to be a football player. He also was raised to be a winner in every aspect of life. He has walked that path religiously without misstep, doing the right thing to demonstrate leadership and commitment to impacting lives beyond the playing field.

Peyton Manning sought to master control of the offense and its huddle when he broke in as a rookie in 1998. It was the most direct way to have a quick and lasting impact.

He took the same dedicated approach to the off-the-field aspect of his career, and he has benefited people of all ages. While changing the mindset in the state of Indiana to create a deep football passion, Peyton also improved the lives of children and adults with his hospital and foundation work.

In addition to the Peyton Manning Children's Hospital in Indianapolis, pictured above, he has been involved in diverse initiatives in Louisiana, Tennessee, and Colorado that were funded by his PeyBack Foundation. "I like to say yes more than I say no," Manning says of his foundation work. According to its website, PeyBack "has distributed more than $10 million in programs and grants since 2002, including over $1 million in May 2015 to 144 youth-based organizations."

Peyton Manning waves the green flag at the start of the Indianapolis 500 auto race at Indianapolis Motor Speedway in 2007.

Supporting the Troops

Manning's life-long sense of duty has taken many forms, and one was on display when he visited service personnel on a 2012 goodwill tour. Peyton was a part of a small NFL contingent that toured Spain, Italy, Asia, Afghanistan, Germany, and a sea vessel. Manning mixed with troops and, in addition to autographing a spent mortar shell, had another first. "I have thrown footballs in lots of place. Boats, prison, schools, military bases, hospitals, golf course fairways, malls, birthday parties, bar mitzvahs, Mardi Gras floats, French Quarter, etc., but I ain't never thrown a football in an airplane. And I am not talking about little three-yard lob passes. I was throwing 35-yard bullets."

Always known for honor, integrity, grit and the right stuff, Manning brightened lives on that trip as he had done for children and adults on and off the field his whole career.

SEPTEMBER 20, 2005

Peyton Manning took part in groundbreaking ceremonies for construction of the 70,000-seat retractable-roof stadium in Indianapolis on Tuesday, September 20, 2005. Others participating in the ceremony were, from left, Indiana Black Expo president Joyce Rogers, Indiana governor Mitch Daniels, Colts owner Jim Irsay, NCAA president Myles Brand, and Indianapolis mayor Bart Peterson. The stadium had its ribbon-cutting ceremony August 16, 2008, and officially opened to the public on August 24, 2008. Officially named Lucas Oil Stadium, it is often affectionately referred to as "The House that Manning Built."

Peyton has been honored for his community involvement by receiving the Byron "Whizzer" White Humanitarian Award (2004), which is "the highest honor the NFL Players Association can bestow on a player"; the Walter Payton NFL Man of the Year Award (2005), which "recognizes an NFL player for his excellence on and off the field"; and the Bart Starr Award (2015), which is annually awarded to a player who "exemplifies character and leadership on and off the field."

"If you want a read on Manning's true impact, look at Lucas Oil Stadium and the Peyton Manning Children's Hospital. They wouldn't exist without him. . . He made Indianapolis a better place to live."
—Phil Richards, Indianapolis Star

Manning and his record-setting 2004 receivers—Brandon Stokley, Marvin Harrison and Reggie Wayne—are symbols of how the Colts have woven their way into the community and its consciousness. Through service work and field performance alongside Jim Irsay and Bill Polian, the team transformed Indiana into a football hotbed.

"Peyton Manning was perceived to be an extraordinary talent when the Colts drafted him, but no one knew he would be an even greater asset to the community. It is difficult to imagine another superstar doing more for his city on and off the field than Peyton."
—John Bansch, former columnist for the Indianapolis Star

OVER TIME

MANNING BY THE NUMBERS

Peyton Manning capped his eye-popping career statistics by becoming the only starting quarterback in history to win Super Bowls with two teams. While numbers never tell the whole story, his stats are an indelible part of the Manning legacy.

PEYTON MANNING

18

quarterback

6-5 • **230** • **18 Years** • **Tennessee**

Born: March 24, 1976, in New Orleans

High School: Isidore Newman High School, New Orleans

NFL Games Played/Started: 266/265 • **Postseason GP/GS:** 27/27

18's Trophy Case

NFL MVP (5) 2003-04, '08-09, '13

Super Bowl XLI MVP 2006

All-Decade Team 2000s

Pro Bowls (14) 1999-2000, '02-10, '12-14

Pro Bowl MVP 2004

All-Pro (1st Team) (7) 2003-05, '08-09, '12-13

All-Pro (2nd Team) (3) 1999-2000, '06

Comeback Player of the Year 2012

Peyton Manning's career statistics are reprinted courtesy of the Denver Broncos.

MANNING AT A GLANCE:

- An 18th-year quarterback and the NFL's only five-time Most Valuable Player whose 14 Pro Bowl selections are tied for the most in league history.

- Stands as the leader in every significant passing category, including attempts (9,380), completions (6,125), passing yards (71,940) and passing touchdowns (539).

- Became the only quarterback in NFL history to lead multiple teams (Indianapolis—2006; Denver—2015) to Super Bowl titles with Denver's 24-10 victory over Carolina in Super Bowl 50.

- Earned his NFL-record 200th victory (regular and postseason) in Super Bowl 50, passing Pro Football Hall of Fame quarterback Brett Favre.

- Started 9-of-10 games played and all three postseason contests for Denver in 2015, playing a key role in the team's fourth consecutive AFC West title and second Super Bowl appearance since he joined the team in 2012.

- Helped his team to the postseason for an NFL-quarterback record 15 times and is the only signal-caller to pilot multiple teams to multiple Super Bowls (Indianapolis—2006, '09; Denver—2013, '15).

- Owns 186 regular-season wins, tied for the most by a quarterback in NFL history (Brett Favre).

- Joined Favre as the only quarterbacks in league annals to earn a victory against each of the 32 current NFL franchises and throw for 70,000 yards in a career.

- Orchestrated the most career game-winning drives in the fourth quarter or overtime (55) since the 1970 NFL merger.

- Named AFC Offensive Player of the Week on 27 occasions while being selected as AFC Offensive Player of the Month eight times—both NFL records.

- Posted at least 300 yards passing in 102 total games (93 reg. season, 9 postseason) and three or more touchdowns in an NFL-best 99 combined games (93 reg. season, 6 postseason).
- Led the NFL in wins (38), touchdown passes (131) and completion percentage (67.7) in his first three seasons (2012-14) with the Broncos after spending the first 14 years (1998-2011) of his career with the Indianapolis Colts.
- Passed Favre for the most passing touchdowns in pro football history on Oct. 19, 2014, and for the most passing yards in pro football history on Nov. 15, 2015.
- Recorded his 14th career 4,000-yard passing season in 2014 to represent the most in NFL history.
- Threw his 100th touchdown as a Bronco in his 35th game with the club (at Seattle, 9/21/14) to become the fastest player in NFL history to reach 100 touchdown passes with a team.
- Named MVP by the Associated Press for the fifth time in his career in 2013 and was recognized as Sports Illustrated's Sportsman of the Year after setting league single-season records for passing yards (5,477) and touchdown passes (55) while directing the highest-scoring offense (606 pts.) in NFL history.
- Chosen as NFL Comeback Player of the Year by the Associated Press in 2012 and finished as the runner-up for MVP following his first season with the Broncos in which he led the team to its second consecutive AFC West title and the AFC's No. 1 seed.
- Selected to the NFL's All-Decade Team for the 2000s as chosen by the Pro Football Hall of Fame Selection Committee.
- Voted Super Bowl XLI MVP (2006 season) after leading the Colts to their first World Championship since 1970 in a 29-17 win over the Bears.
- Recognized for his community involvement by receiving the Byron "Whizzer" White Humanitarian Award (2004), the Walter Payton NFL Man of the Year Award (2005) and the Bart Starr Award (2015).

- His jersey No. 18 is technically retired by Denver, but the late Broncos Ring of Fame quarterback Frank Tripucka gave Manning his blessing to wear the number in 2012.
- Started 45-of-48 games at the University of Tennessee and set 33 school records, eight Southeastern Conference marks and two NCAA standards.
- Led the Volunteers to an SEC Championship as a senior in 1997 and finished as the Heisman trophy runner-up and a consensus All-American.
- Joined the Broncos as a free agent on March 20, 2012.
- Selected by Indianapolis in the first round (1st overall) of the 1998 NFL Draft.

CAREER TRANSACTIONS: Signed by Indianapolis as a draft choice 7/29/98; Released by Indianapolis 3/7/12; Signed by Denver 3/20/12; Retired from the NFL, 3/7/16.

Peyton Manning with Gary Kubiak and John Elway
on the day Manning announced his retirement.

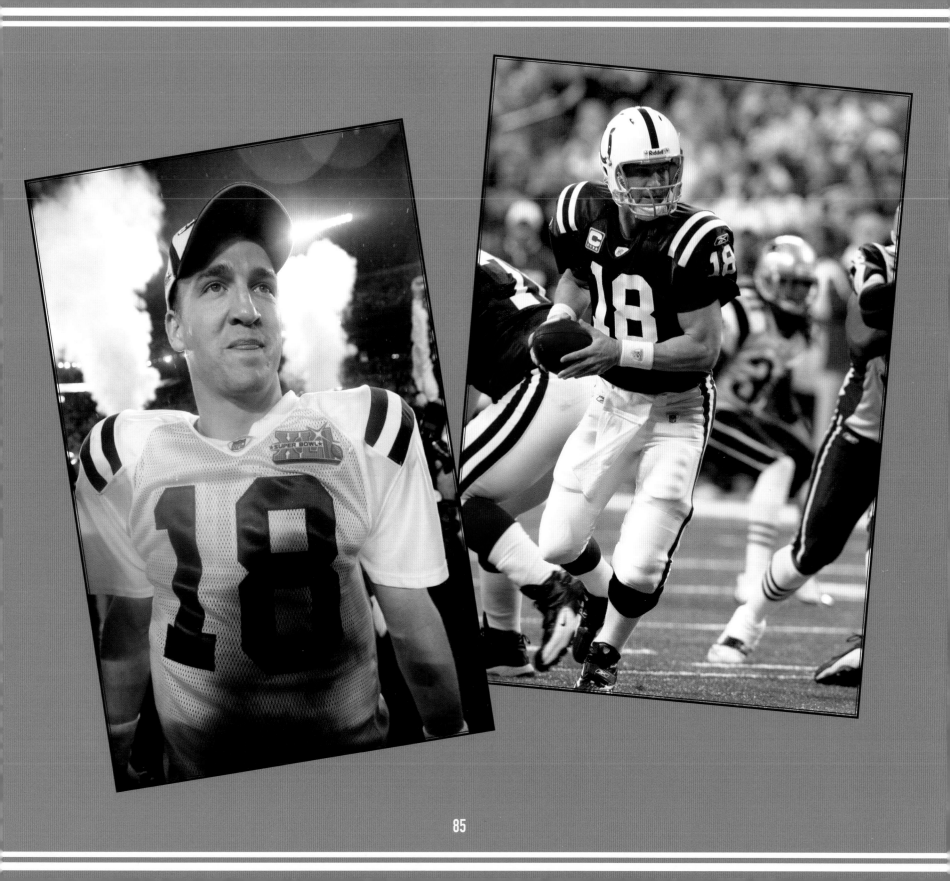

Manning's Regular Season Record

PASSING

Year	Club	G	S	Att.	Comp.	Pct.	Yds.	Yds./Att.	TD	%	Int.	%	LG	Sack/Yds.	Rtg.
1998	Indianapolis	16	16	575	326	56.7	3,739	6.5	26	4.5	28	4.9	78t	22/109	71.2
1999	Indianapolis	16	16	533	331	62.1	4,135	7.8	26	4.9	15	2.8	80t	14/116	90.7
2000	Indianapolis	16	16	571	357	62.5	4,413	7.7	33	5.8	15	2.6	78t	20/131	94.7
2001	Indianapolis	16	16	547	343	62.7	4,131	7.6	26	4.8	23	4.2	86t	29/232	84.1
2002	Indianapolis	16	16	591	392	66.3	4,200	7.1	27	4.6	19	3.2	69	23/145	88.8
2003	Indianapolis	16	16	566	379	67.0	4,267	7.5	29	5.1	10	1.8	79t	18/107	99.0
2004	Indianapolis	16	16	497	336	67.6	4,557	9.2	49	9.9	10	2.0	80t	13/101	121.1
2005	Indianapolis	16	16	453	305	67.3	3,747	8.3	28	6.2	10	2.2	80t	17/81	104.1
2006	Indianapolis	16	16	557	362	65.0	4,397	7.9	31	5.6	9	1.6	68t	14/86	101.0
2007	Indianapolis	16	16	515	337	65.4	4,040	7.8	31	6.0	14	2.7	73t	21/124	98.0
2008	Indianapolis	16	16	555	371	66.8	4,002	7.2	27	4.9	12	2.2	75	14/86	95.0
2009	Indianapolis	16	16	571	393	68.8	4,500	7.9	33	5.8	16	2.8	80t	10/74	99.9
2010	Indianapolis	16	16	679	450	66.3	4,700	6.9	33	4.9	17	2.5	73t	16/91	91.9
2011	Indianapolis	0	0	0	0	0.0	0	0.0	0	0	0	0	—	0/0	0.0
2012	Denver	16	16	583	400	68.6	4,659	8.0	37	6.3	11	1.9	71t	21/137	105.8
2013	Denver	16	16	659	450	68.3	5,477	8.3	55	8.3	10	1.5	78t	18/120	115.1
2014	Denver	16	16	597	395	66.2	4,727	7.9	39	6.5	15	2.5	86t	17/118	101.5
2015	Denver	10	9	331	198	59.8	2,249	6.8	9	2.7	17	5.1	75t	16/95	67.9
CAREER TOTALS		**266**	**265**	**9,380**	**6,125**	**65.3**	**71,940**	**7.7**	**539**	**5.7**	**251**	**2.7**	**86t**	**303/1,953**	**96.5**
BRONCOS TOTALS		**58**	**57**	**2,170**	**1,443**	**66.5**	**17,112**	**7.9**	**140**	**6.5**	**53**	**2.4**	**86t**	**72/470**	**101.7**

		RUSHING						**SCORING**					
Year	Club	Att.	Yds.	Avg.	LG	TD	TD	TDr	TDp	TDrt	2pt	Pts.
1998	Indianapolis	15	62	4.1	15	0	0	0	0	0	0	0
1999	Indianapolis	35	73	2.1	13	2	2	2	0	0	0	12
2000	Indianapolis	37	116	3.1	14	1	1	1	0	0	0	6
2001	Indianapolis	35	157	4.5	33t	4	4	4	0	0	0	24
2002	Indianapolis	38	148	3.9	13	2	2	2	0	0	0	12
2003	Indianapolis	28	26	0.9	10	0	0	0	0	0	0	0
2004	Indianapolis	25	38	1.5	19	0	0	0	0	0	0	0
2005	Indianapolis	33	45	1.4	12	0	0	0	0	0	0	0
2006	Indianapolis	23	36	1.6	12	4	4	4	0	0	0	24
2007	Indianapolis	20	-5	-0.3	4	3	3	3	0	0	0	18
2008	Indianapolis	20	21	1.1	12	1	1	1	0	0	0	6
2009	Indianapolis	19	-13	-0.7	3	0	0	0	0	0	0	0
2010	Indianapolis	18	18	1.0	27	0	0	0	0	0	0	0
2011	Indianapolis	0	0	0.0	—	0	0	0	0	0	0	0
2012	Denver	23	6	0.3	10	0	0	0	0	0	0	0
2013	Denver	32	-31	-1.0	1t	1	1	1	0	0	0	6
2014	Denver	24	-24	-1.0	4	0	0	0	0	0	0	0
2015	Denver	6	-6	-1.0	-1	0	0	0	0	0	0	0
CAREER TOTALS		**431**	**667**	**1.5**	**33t**	**18**	**18**	**18**	**0**	**0**	**0**	**108**
BRONCOS TOTALS		**85**	**-55**	**-0.6**	**10**	**1**	**1**	**1**	**0**	**0**	**0**	**6**

ADDITIONAL STATISTICS: *Receptions — (1- -2, 2.0 avg., 2 LG), Fumble recoveries — 1999 (2), 2000 (1), 2001 (3), 2002 (2), 2003 (4), 2004 (3), 2007 (3), 2010 (1), TOTAL (19).*

Manning Named NFL Most Valuable Player Five Times

MOST NFL MVP AWARDS, NFL HISTORY

	Player	MVPs	Years Selected
1.	**Peyton Manning**	**5**	**2003-04, '08-09, '13**
2.	Brett Favre	3	1995-97
	Johnny Unitas	3	1959, '64, '67
	Jim Brown	3	1957-58, 1965
5.	Tom Brady	2	2007, '10
	Kurt Warner	2	1999, 2001
	Steve Young	2	1992, '94
	Joe Montana	2	1989-90
	Aaron Rodgers	2	2011, '14

MOST MVP AWARDS, MAJOR U.S. SPORTS

	Player	League	MVPs
1.	Wayne Gretzky	NHL	9
2.	Barry Bonds	MLB	7
3.	Kareem Abdul-Jabbar	NBA	6
	Gordie Howe	NHL	6
5.	**Peyton Manning**	**NFL**	**5**
	Michael Jordan	NBA	5
	Bill Russell	NBA	5

ALL-TIME PRO FOOTBALL PASSING LEADERS

PASSING YARDS

No.	Player	Yards
1.	**Peyton Manning***	**71,940**
2.	Brett Favre	71,838
3.	Dan Marino	61,361
4.	Drew Brees*	60,903
5.	Tom Brady*	58,028

PASS ATTEMPTS

No.	Player	Att.
1.	Brett Favre	10,169
2.	**Peyton Manning***	**9,380**
3.	Dan Marino	8,358
4.	Drew Brees*	8,085
5.	Tom Brady*	7,792

* active player

ALL-TIME PRO FOOTBALL PASSING LEADERS

TOUCHDOWN PASSES

No.	Player	TDs
1.	**Peyton Manning***	**539**
2.	Brett Favre	508
3.	Tom Brady*	428
	Drew Brees*	428
5.	Dan Marino	420

PASS COMPLETIONS

No.	Player	Comp.
1.	Brett Favre	6,300
2.	**Peyton Manning***	**6,125**
3.	Drew Brees*	5,365
4.	Dan Marino	4,967
5.	Tom Brady*	4,953

* active player

MANNING ACCUSTOMED TO WINNING

MOST VICTORIES BY A STARTING QUARTERBACK, ALL-TIME (REGULAR SEASON ONLY)

Player	W-L-T	Pct.
1. **Peyton Manning***	**186-79-0**	**.702**
2. Brett Favre	186-114-0	.623
3. Tom Brady*	172-51-0	.771
4. John Elway	148-82-1	.643
5. Dan Marino	147-93-0	.613

* active player

MANNING SELECTED TO 14 PRO BOWLS

MOST PRO BOWL SELECTIONS BY A QUARTERBACK, NFL HISTORY

Player	No.	Seasons Selected
1. **Peyton Manning**	**14**	**1999-2000, '02-10, '12-14**
2. Brett Favre	11	1992-93, '95-97, 2001-03, '07-09
3. Tom Brady	11	2001, '04-05, '07, '09-15
4. John Elway	9	1986-89, '91-94, '96-98
Dan Marino	9	1983-87, '91-92, '94-95
Warren Moon	9	1988-95, '97

MANNING'S RECORD-BREAKING 2013 SEASON

PEYTON MANNING'S NFL SINGLE-SEASON STATISTICAL RECORDS SET IN 2013

Category	No.	Old Record
Passing Yards	5,477	5,476 (Drew Brees, 2011)
400-Yard Passing Games	4*	4 (Dan Marino, 1984)
Passing Touchdowns	55	51 (Tom Brady, 2007)
Four-Touchdown Games	9	6 (Manning, 2004 / Dan Marino, 1984)
Most TDs w/o INT to start season	20	17 (Milt Plum, 1960)
Passing First Downs	289	278 (Drew Brees, 2011)

*tied record

WHERE MANNING RANKS IN NFL HISTORY

Regular Season	No.	Active Rank	All-Time Rank
Wins (QBs)	186	1	T-1
Attempts	9,380	1	2
Completions	6,125	1	2
Passing Yards	71,940	1	1
Passing TDs	539	1	1
Passer Rtg. (min. 1,500 att.)	96.5	4	5
300-yard Passing Games	93	2	2
Games with 3+ Passing TDs	93	1	1
Games with 100+ Passer Rtg.	112	1	1
3,000-yard Passing Seasons	16	1	2
4,000-yard Passing Seasons	14	1	1
Seasons with 25+ Passing TDs	16	1	1
Postseason	**No.**	**Active Rank**	**All-Time Rank**
Postseason Berths (QBs)	15	1	1
Wins (QBs)	14	2	4
Attempts	1,027	2	2
Completions	649	2	2
Passing Yards	7,198	2	2
Passing TDs	40	2	4
Passer Rtg. (min. 150 att.)	87.4	9	16
300-yard Passing Games	9	T-1	T-1
Games with 3+ Passing TDs	6	2	3t
Games with 100+ Passer Rtg.	6	2t	7t

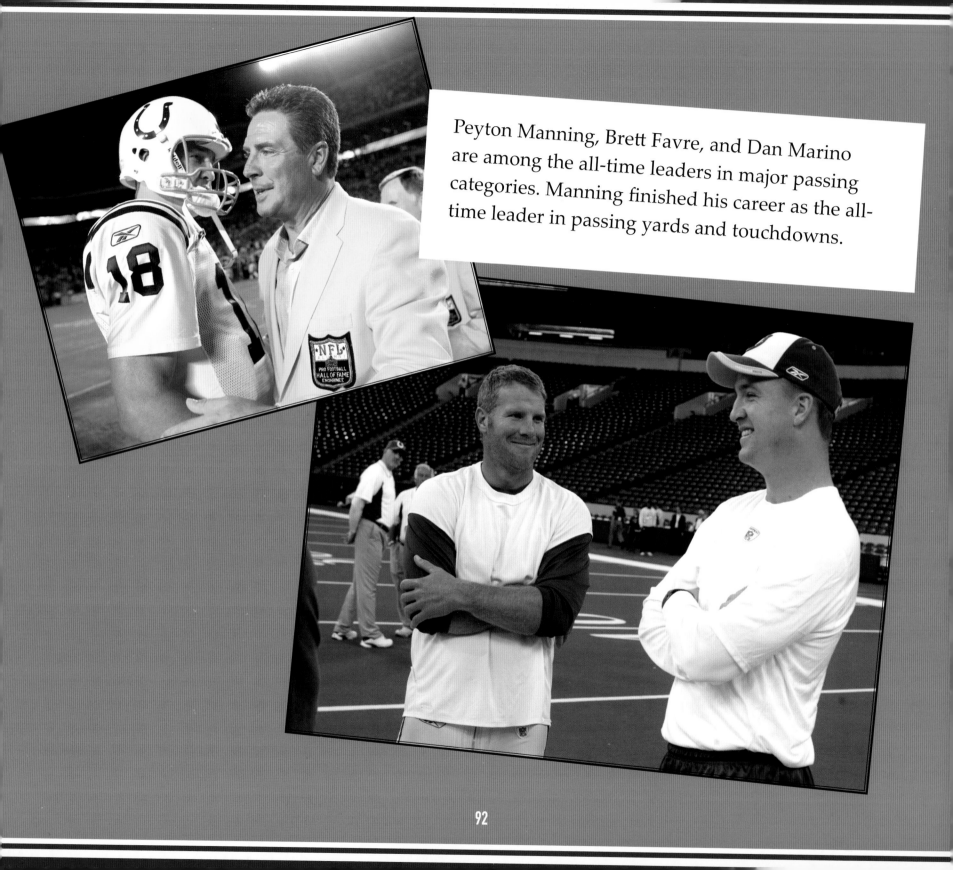

Peyton Manning, Brett Favre, and Dan Marino are among the all-time leaders in major passing categories. Manning finished his career as the all-time leader in passing yards and touchdowns.

MANNING OWNS NFL RECORD FOR TOUCHDOWN PASSES

MOST TOUCHDOWN PASSES, NFL HISTORY

	Player	No.
1.	**Peyton Manning**	**539**
2.	Brett Favre	508
3.	Tom Brady	428
	Drew Brees	428
5.	Dan Marino	420

PEYTON MANNING'S TOUCHDOWN MILESTONES

TD	Opp. (Date)	Scoring Play
1	vs. Mia. (9/6/98)	Marvin Harrison (6 yds.)
100	vs. Mia. (11/11/01)	Marvin Harrison (11 yds.)
200	at Chi. (11/21/04)	Reggie Wayne (35 yds.)
300	at Bal. (12/9/07)	Joseph Addai (19 yds.)
400	vs. Pit. (9/9/12)	Demaryius Thomas (71 yds.)
500	vs. Ari. (10/5/14)	Julius Thomas (7 yds.)
509	vs. S.F. (10/19/14)	Demaryius Thomas (8 yds.)

MANNING LED TWO FRANCHISES TO SUPER BOWL

STARTING QBS TO LEAD MULTIPLE TEAMS TO THE SUPER BOWL

Quarterback	First Team	Second Team
Craig Morton	Dallas (1970)	Denver (1977)
Kurt Warner	St. Louis (1999, 2001)	Arizona (2008)
Peyton Manning	**Indianapolis (2006, '09)**	**Denver (2013, '15)**

Peyton Manning was selected to the Pro Bowl 14 times during his career, the most by a quarterback in NFL history.

Manning's 300-yard passing GAMES (102)

denotes win (Manning's teams were 67-35, including the postseason, when he recorded more than 300 passing yards in a game.)

Date	Opponent	Yds.	Date	Opponent	Yds.
9/6/1998	vs. Miami	302	9/13/2009	vs. Jacksonville*	301
9/27/1998	vs. New Orleans	309	9/21/2009	at Miami*	303
11/29/1998	at Baltimore	357	9/27/2009	at Arizona*	379
12/20/1998	at Seattle	335	10/4/2009	vs. Seattle*	353
9/26/1999	at San Diego*	404	10/11/2009	at Tennessee*	309
10/31/1999	vs. Dallas*	313	11/1/2009	vs. San Francisco*	347
9/10/2000	vs. Oakland	367	11/8/2009	vs. Houston*	318
9/25/2000	vs. Jacksonville*	440	11/15/2009	vs. New England*	327
10/8/2000	at New England	334	12/17/2009	at Jacksonville*	308
11/5/2000	at Chicago	302	1/24/2010	vs. N.Y. Jets*^	377
12/3/2000	at N.Y. Jets	339	2/7/2010	vs. New Orleans^	333
9/23/2001	vs. Buffalo*	421	9/12/2010	at Houston	433
10/21/2001	vs. New England	335	9/26/2010	at Denver*	325
11/25/2001	vs. San Francisco	370	10/3/2010	at Jacksonville	352
12/2/2001	at Baltimore	310	10/17/2010	at Washington*	307
12/16/2001	vs. Atlanta*	325	11/21/2010	at New England	396
10/21/2002	at Pittsburgh	304	12/5/2010	vs. Dallas	365
11/3/2002	vs. Tennessee	327	12/9/2010	at Tennessee*	319
11/10/2002	at Philadelphia*	319	9/23/2012	vs. Houston	330
12/22/2002	vs. N.Y. Giants	365	9/30/2012	vs. Oakland*	338
9/28/2003	at New Orleans*	314	10/7/2012	at New England	337
10/6/2003	at Tampa Bay*	386	10/15/2012	at San Diego*	309
11/9/2003	at Jacksonville	347	10/28/2012	vs. New Orleans*	305
11/16/2003	vs. N.Y. Jets*	401	11/11/2012	at Carolina*	301
1/4/2004	vs. Denver*^	377	12/6/2012	at Oakland*	310
1/11/2004	at Kansas City*^	304	12/23/2012	vs. Cleveland*	339

Date	Opponent	Yards		Date	Opponent	Yards
9/26/2004	vs. Green Bay*	393		12/30/2012	vs. Kansas City*	304
10/24/2004	vs. Jacksonville	368		9/5/2013	vs. Baltimore*	462
10/31/2004	at Kansas City	472		9/15/2013	at N.Y. Giants*	307
11/14/2004	vs. Houston*	320		9/23/2013	vs. Oakland*	374
12/5/2004	vs. Tennessee*	425		9/29/2013	vs. Philadelphia*	327
12/26/2004	vs. San Diego*	383		10/5/2013	at Dallas*	414
1/9/2005	vs. Denver*^	458		10/20/2013	at Indianapolis	386
11/7/2005	at New England*	321		10/27/2013	vs. Washington*	354
11/20/2005	at Cincinnati*	365		11/10/2013	at San Diego*	330
12/11/2005	at Jacksonville*	324		11/17/2013	vs. Kansas City*	323
12/18/2005	vs. San Diego	336		12/1/2013	at Kansas City*	403
9/17/2006	vs. Houston*	400		12/8/2013	vs. Tennessee*	397
10/22/2006	vs. Washington*	342		12/22/2013	at Houston*	400
10/29/2006	at Denver*	345		1/19/2013	vs. New England^*	400
11/5/2006	at New England*	326		9/21/14	at Seattle	303
12/3/2006	at Tennessee	351		10/5/14	vs. Arizona*	479
12/10/2006	at Jacksonville	313		10/19/14	vs. San Francisco*	318
1/21/2007	vs. New England*^	349		11/2/14	at New England	438
9/16/2007	at Tennessee*	312		11/9/14	at Oakland*	340
11/11/2007	at San Diego	328		11/16/14	at St. Louis	389
12/23/2007	vs. Houston*	311		12/22/14	at Cincinnati	311
1/13/2008	vs. San Diego^	402		9/27/15	at Detroit*	324
9/14/2008	at Minnesota*	311		11/1/15	vs. Green Bay*	340
11/16/2008	vs. Houston*	320		^Playoff Game		
12/14/2008	vs. Detroit*	318				
12/18/2008	at Jacksonville*	364				
1/3/2009	at San Diego^	310				

11/7/99	Kansas City	16-17	25-17	7t Manning run	10:49	6-54/3:04	2-3-17 pass/2-10 rush, 7t

Manning's Postseason Record

PASSING

Year	Club	G	S	Att.	Comp.	Pct.	Yds.	Yds./Att.	TD	%	Int.	%	LG	Sack/Yds.	Rtg.
1999	Indianapolis	1	1	42	19	44.2	227	5.3	0	0.0	0	0.0	33	0/0	60.9
2000	Indianapolis	1	1	32	17	53.1	194	6.1	1	3.1	0	0.0	30	0/0	82.0
2002	Indianapolis	1	1	31	14	45.2	137	4.4	0	0.0	2	6.5	17	1/13	31.3
2003	Indianapolis	3	3	103	67	65.0	918	8.9	9	8.7	4	3.9	87t	5/41	106.4
2004	Indianapolis	2	2	75	54	72.0	696	9.3	4	5.3	2	2.7	49	2/12	107.4
2005	Indianapolis	1	1	38	22	57.9	290	7.6	1	2.6	0	0.0	50t	5/43	90.9
2006	Indianapolis	4	4	153	97	63.4	1,034	6.8	3	2.0	7	4.6	53t	6/41	70.5
2007	Indianapolis	1	1	48	33	68.8	402	8.4	3	6.3	2	4.2	55t	0/0	97.7
2008	Indianapolis	1	1	42	25	59.5	310	7.4	1	2.4	0	0.0	72t	1/8	90.4
2009	Indianapolis	3	3	128	87	68.0	956	7.5	6	4.7	2	1.6	46	4/30	98.9
2010	Indianapolis	1	1	26	18	69.2	225	8.7	1	3.8	0	0.0	57t	1/6	108.7
2012	Denver	1	1	43	28	65.1	290	6.7	3	7.0	2	4.7	32	3/17	88.3
2013	Denver	3	3	128	91	71.1	910	7.1	5	3.9	3	2.3	37	1/1	94.2
2014	Denver	1	1	46	26	56.5	211	4.6	1	2.2	0	0.0	32	2/11	75.5
2015	Denver	3	3	92	51	55.4	539	5.9	2	2.2	1	1.1	34	9/75	75.4
CAREER TOTALS		**27**	**27**	**1,027**	**649**	**63.2**	**7,338**	**7.1**	**40**	**3.9**	**25**	**2.4**	**87t**	**40/298**	**87.4**
BRONCOS TOTALS		**8**	**8**	**309**	**196**	**63.4**	**1,950**	**6.3**	**11**	**3.6**	**6**	**1.9**	**37**	**15/104**	**85.0**

RUSHING | SCORING

Year	Club	Att.	Yds.	Avg.	LG	TD		TD	TDr	TDp	TDrt	2pt	Pts.
1999	Indianapolis	3	22	7.3	15t	1		1	1	0	0	0	6
2000	Indianapolis	1	-2	-2.0	-2	0		0	0	0	0	0	0
2002	Indianapolis	1	2	2.0	2	0		0	0	0	0	0	0

		RUSHING								SCORING				
Year	Club	Att.	Yds.	Avg.	LG	TD		TD	TDr	TDp	TDrt	2pt	Pts.
2003	Indianapolis	4	3	0.8	3	0		0	0	0	0	0	0
2004	Indianapolis	2	8	4.0	7	1		1	1	0	0	0	6
2005	Indianapolis	0	0	0.0	—	0		0	0	0	0	0	0
2006	Indianapolis	8	3	0.4	7	1		1	1	0	0	0	6
2007	Indianapolis	1	-6	-6.0	-6	0		0	0	0	0	0	0
2008	Indianapolis	1	-1	-1.0	-1	0		0	0	0	0	0	0
2009	Indianapolis	3	-2	-0.7	0	0		0	0	0	0	0	0
2010	Indianapolis	0	0	0.0	—	0		0	0	0	0	0	0
2012	Denver	1	-1	-1.0	-1	0		0	0	0	0	0	0
2013	Denver	3	-2	-1.0	-1	0		0	0	0	0	0	0
2014	Denver	0	0	0.0	—	0		0	0	0	0	0	0
2015	Denver	5	10	2.0	12	0		0	0	0	0	0	0
CAREER TOTALS		**33**	**34**	**1.0**	**15t**	**3**		**3**	**3**	**0**	**0**	**0**	**18**
BRONCOS TOTALS		**9**	**7**	**0.8**	**12**	**0**		**0**	**0**	**0**	**0**	**0**	**0**

ADDITIONAL STATISTICS: *Fumble recoveries — 2003 (1), TOTAL (1).*

MANNING'S SINGLE-GAME HIGHS

(Postseason in parentheses)

Pass attempts — 59 vs. Tennessee, 12/8/13 (49 vs. Seattle, 2/2/14). **Pass completions** — 40 at Houston, 9/12/10 (34 vs. Seattle, 2/2/14). **Passing yards** — 479 vs. Arizona, 10/5/14 (458 vs. Denver, 1/9/05). **Completion percentage (min. 10 att.)** — 89.3% (25-28) at Oakland, 12/29/13 (84.6% (22-26) vs. Denver, 1/4/04). **Touchdown passes** — 7 vs. Baltimore, 9/5/13 (5 vs. Denver, 1/4/04). **Longest pass completion** — 86t, twice, last vs. Arizona, 10/5/14 (87t vs. Denver, 1/4/04). **Rushing attempts** — 7 vs. Buffalo, 9/23/01 (3, twice, last at Baltimore, 1/13/07). **Rushing yards** — 44 at Buffalo, 11/4/01 (22 vs. Tennessee, 1/16/00). **Longest rush** — 33t at Buffalo, 11/4/01 (15t vs. Tennessee, 1/16/00). **Rushing touchdowns** — 1, 18 times, last at Dallas, 10/6/13 (1, three times, last vs. New England, 1/21/07)

PEYTON MANNING'S NFL SPLITS

Regular Season Only

	Gms.	W	L	Att.	Cmp.	Pct.	Yds.	TD	INT	LG	S/Yds.	Rtg.
Denver	8	6	2	250	155	62.0	1,655	15	5	63	5/30	93.0
Kansas City	13	12	1	461	284	61.6	3,635	28	9	77	17/115	98.4
Oakland	11	9	2	404	278	68.8	3,162	28	11	63t	13/81	103.8
San Diego	13	9	4	518	331	63.9	3,845	28	19	74t	19/126	89.0
AFC West	**45**	**36**	**9**	**1,633**	**1,048**	**64.2**	**12,2297**	**99**	**44**	**77**	**54/351**	**95.9**
Buffalo	12	8	4	358	223	62.3	2,518	13	12	60t	9/66	81.4
Miami	13	6	7	436	272	62.4	3,214	22	18	80t	19/142	84.4
New England	19	6	13	723	453	62.7	5,316	43	26	78t	26/179	89.8
N.Y. Jets	12	8	4	427	269	63.0	2,932	16	11	54	15/101	84.9
AFC East	**56**	**28**	**28**	**1,944**	**1,217**	**62.6**	**13,980**	**94**	**67**	**80t**	**69/488**	**86.0**
Baltimore	11	9	2	385	247	64.2	3,114	25	6	78t	21/159	104.4
Cincinnati	9	8	1	316	209	66.1	2,429	22	9	69	7/28	100.6
Cleveland	6	6	0	207	138	66.7	1,456	5	7	51	2/10	80.9
Pittsburgh	4	3	1	139	87	62.6	1,042	8	4	80t	8/40	92.7
AFC North	**30**	**26**	**4**	**1,047**	**675**	**64.5**	**8,061**	**60**	**24**	**80t**	**38/227**	**98.2**
Houston	20	17	3	745	510	68.5	5,852	48	8	80t	27/159	108.9
Indianapolis	2	1	1	85	51	60.0	655	6	1	49	5/31	102.8
Jacksonville	20	15	5	710	462	65.1	5,538	40	14	76t	15/105	99.4
Tennessee	19	14	5	638	448	70.2	4,956	35	13	68t	14/90	102.8
AFC South	**61**	**47**	**14**	**2,164**	**1,485**	**68.6**	**17,387**	**129**	**36**	**80t**	**61/385**	**103.1**
AFC Totals	**194**	**138**	**56**	**6,871**	**4,460**	**64.9**	**51,935**	**384**	**174**	**80t**	**225/1,468**	**95.7**
Arizona	3	3	0	84	56	66.7	863	8	3	86t	2/3	117.3
St. Louis	4	2	2	148	94	63.5	1,010	6	3	42t	6/41	88.5
San Francisco	5	3	2	186	125	67.2	1,521	9	6	61t	8/50	94.8
Seattle*	5	2	3	171	114	66.7	1,388	6	3	53	4/13	95.8
NFC West	**17**	**10**	**7**	**589**	**389**	**66.0**	**4,782**	**29**	**15**	**86t**	**20/107**	**93.2**
Dallas	5	3	2	201	140	69.7	1,598	11	8	57	3/20	94.9
N.Y. Giants	5	4	1	191	125	65.4	1,440	11	4	57t	4/25	98.5

	Gms.	W	L	Att.	Cmp.	Pct.	Yds.	TD	INT	LG	S/Yds.	Rtg.
Philadelphia	5	4	1	154	107	69.5	1,358	12	3	80t	5/32	114.6
Washington	5	4	1	186	124	66.7	1,515	14	6	57t	7/49	103.2
NFC East	**20**	**15**	**5**	**732**	**496**	**67.8**	**5,911**	**48**	**21**	**80t**	**19/126**	**102.1**
Chicago	3	1	2	116	73	62.9	770	7	2	35t	4/38	95.1
Detroit	3	3	0	98	73	74.5	842	10	2	39	2/10	125.5
Green Bay	3	1	2	126	74	58.7	916	8	3	36t	4/27	92.6
Minnesota	3	3	0	107	74	69.2	862	9	3	75	3/19	109.6
NFC North	**12**	**8**	**4**	**447**	**294**	**65.8**	**3,390**	**34**	**10**	**75**	**13/94**	**104.5**
Atlanta	5	3	2	161	113	70.2	1,287	14	7	37t	8/57	104.7
Carolina	4	2	2	136	81	59.6	1,074	5	3	59t	6/24	87.7
New Orleans	5	3	2	145	97	66.9	1,478	14	4	86t	5/26	121.0
Tampa Bay	3	3	0	122	90	73.8	881	7	3	52	1/5	102.5
NFC South	**17**	**11**	**6**	**564**	**381**	**67.6**	**4,720**	**40**	**17**	**86t**	**20/112**	**101.7**
NFC Totals	**73**	**43**	**21**	**2,263**	**1,517**	**67.0**	**18,187**	**149**	**62**	**86t**	**69/433**	**102.0**
NFL Totals	**258**	**181**	**77**	**9,134**	**5,977**	**65.4**	**70,122**	**533**	**236**	**86t**	**294/1,901**	**97.3**
Home	129	99	30	4,481	2,960	66.1	35,049	276	102	86t	140/857	100.8
Road	129	82	47	4,653	3,017	64.8	35,073	257	134	86t	154/1,044	93.9
Wins	181	181	0	6,143	4,141	67.4	49,242	408	111	86t	179/1,163	106.3
Losses	77	0	77	2,991	1,836	61.4	20,880	125	125	86t	115/738	78.8
Grass	111	81	30	4,012	2,652	66.1	30,912	239	101	86t	130/859	98.6
Turf	149	101	49	5,122	3,325	64.9	39,210	294	135	86t	164/1,042	96.2
Outdoors	144	102	42	5,272	3,444	65.3	39,993	297	133	86t	170/1,137	96.4
Domes	114	79	35	3,862	2,533	65.6	30,129	236	103	86t	124/764	98.5
Sundays	226	157	69	8,035	5,227	65.1	61,129	454	210	86t	253/1,650	95.9
Mondays	18	13	5	640	435	68.0	5,030	38	20	80t	22/116	98.2
Thursdays	13	11	2	447	306	68.5	3,847	41	6	78t	19/135	120.0
Saturdays	1	0	1	12	9	75.0	116	0	0	39	0/0	104.9
September	55	40	15	1,974	1,276	64.6	15,642	118	49	80t	68/431	98.5
October	59	42	16	2,062	1,382	67.0	16,325	132	50	86t	60/367	102.2
November	69	47	22	2,626	1,680	64.0	18,882	145	79	86t	91/639	91.2
December	70	49	21	2,350	1,562	66.5	18,549	134	56	77	72/450	99.4
January	6	3	3	122	77	63.1	724	4	2	43t	3/14	83.5

Includes two games prior to the 2002 season when Seattle was in the AFC

Manning's career game-winning drives in 4th qtr. or overtime (54)

Regular font denotes game-winning drive; *Italics denotes comeback drive;* **Bold denotes drives with the Broncos**

Date	Opponent	Down/Tied	Won	Game-Winning Play	Time Left	Drive/T.O.P.	Manning Drive Stats
11/15/98	NY Jets	17-23	24-23	14t pass to Marcus Pollard	0:24	15-80/2:40	8-13-93, 1 TD pass
9/26/99	at San Diego	13-19	27-19	12t Manning run	11:41	8-83/2:47	3-6-46 pass; 12t rush
10/17/99	at NY Jets	13-13	16-13	Vanderjagt 27 FG	0:14	10-35/4:18	2-2-12 pass, 1-(-2 rush)
		10-13		*Vanderjagt 18 FG*	*12:06*	*12-53/4:43*	*4-8-40 pass*
10/31/99	Dallas	21-24	34-24	40t pass to Marvin Harrison	14:55	7-75/3:31	4-7-76, 1 TD pass
11/7/99	Kansas City	16-17	25-17	7t Manning run	10:49	6-54/3:04	2-3-17 pass/2-10 rush, 7t
12/5/99	at Miami	34-34	37-34	Vanderjagt 53 FG	0:00	4-33/0:36	2-2-34 passing
12/19/99	Washington	10-13	24-21	1t pass to Ken Dilger	14:56	7-80/3:11	3-4-40 pass, 1 TD pass
12/26/99	at Cleveland	26-28	29-28	Vanderjagt 21 FG	0:04	11-54/4:08	4-4-23 pass/1-8 rush
		19-28		*2t James run*	*9:54*	*11-77/5:06*	*6-7-53 pass/1-9 rush*
9/3/00	at Kansas City	14-14	27-14	Vanderjagt 23 FG	13:37	9-27/3:56	3-4-16 pass
10/1/00	at Buffalo	15-16	18-16	Vanderjagt 45 FG	0:00	8-42/1:08	3-5-25 pass/1-2 rush
10/22/00	New England	21-23	30-23	3t James run	2:09	6-66/2:22	2-2-13 pass
		14-23		*1t pass to Edgerrin James*	*6:16*	*8-65/3:32*	*6-9-40, 1 TD pass*
10/13/02	Baltimore	19-20	22-20	Vanderjagt 38 FG	0:04	11-60/2:18	5-6-49 pass
11/17/02	Dallas	3-3	20-3	Vanderjagt 32 FG	13:06	12-76/6:53	3-3-31 pass/1-(-1) rush
11/24/02	at Denver	20-20	23-20	Vanderjagt 51 FG	9:22 OT	10-35/5:38	2-3-14 pass
		17-20		*Vanderjagt 54 FG*	*0:03*	*11-44/1:37*	*3-8-27 pass/2-12 rush*
12/15/02	at Cleveland	21-23	28-23	3t Mungro run	6:46	6-86/3:00	2-2-53 pass
		14-23		*3t pass to Marvin Harrison*	*11:30*	*7-57/2:58*	*4-6-49, 1 TD pass*
12/29/02	vs. Jacksonville	13-13	20-13	11t pass to Marcus Pollard	2:26	7-47/2:11	3-3-32 pass, 1 TD pass
		10-13		*Vanderjagt 27 FG*	*5:46*	*16-68/8:09*	*5-9-25 pass/1-8 rush*
9/7/03	at Cleveland	6-6	9-6	Vanderjagt 45 FG	0:01	11-65/2:38	8-10-65 pass
10/6/03	at Tampa Bay	35-35	38-35	Vanderjagt 29 FG	3:47 OT	15-76/6:46	5-9-49 pass

Date	Opponent	Down/Tied	Won	Game-Winning Play	Time Left	Drive/T.O.P.	Manning Drive Stats
		28-35		*1t R. Williams run*	*0:35*	*5-85/1:06*	*2-3-64 pass*
		21-35		*28t pass to Marvin Harrison*	*2:29*	*6-58/1:08*	*5-6-63, 1 TD pass*
		14-35		*3t Mungro run*	*3:37*	*4-12/1:32*	*1-2-6 pass*
11/23/03	at Buffalo	10-14	17-14	1t James run	1:38	16-83/6:00	5-7-55 pass
		3-14		*14t James run*	*10:40*	*9-61/4:11*	*3-4-15 pass*
12/28/03	at Houston	17-17	20-17	Vanderjagt 43 FG	0:00	12-65/2:40	2-4-22 pass/2-8 rush
		10-17		*5t pass to Brandon Stokley*	*3:50*	*1-5/0:05*	*1-1-5, 1 TD pass*
		3-17		*6t James run*	*14:57*	*11-67/5:36*	*3-3-24 pass*
9/19/04	at Tennessee	17-17	31-17	4t James run	7:31	11-80/3:57	4-7-70 pass
		10-17		*1t pass to Marcus Pollard*	*14:56*	*6-80/2:42*	*3-4-57 pass, 1 TD pass*
10/3/04	at Jacksonville	17-17	24-17	3t James run	3:33	13-74/7:04	5-5-33 pass
11/8/04	Minnesota	28-28	31-28	Vanderjagt 35 FG	0:02	9-55/2:52	2-2-23 pass/3-12 rush
12/26/04	San Diego	31-31	34-31	Vanderjagt 30 FG	12:13 OT	5-61/2:47	2-2-58 pass
		23-31		*21t pass to Brandon Stokley*	*0:56*	*9-80/2:46*	*6-8-85, 1 TD pass*
9/18/05	Jacksonville	0-3	10-3	6t Carthon run	8:33	17-88/8:59	3-3-21 pass
10/1/06	at NY Jets	24-28	31-28	1t Manning run	0:50	9-61/1:30	6-8-60 pass/1-1, 1t rush
10/8/06	Tennessee	7-13	14-13	2t pass to Reggie Wayne	5:10	10-43/4:28	4-6-34, 1 TD pass
10/29/06	at Denver	31-31	34-31	Vinatieri 37 FG	0:02	8-62/1:47	5-5-47 pass
		23-28		*19t pass to Reggie Wayne*	*3:35*	*7-80/3:19*	*5-6-75, 1 TD pass*
11/18/07	Kansas City	10-10	13-10	Vinatieri 24 FG	0:03	14-61/6:56	4-4-59 pass/4-(-3) rush
12/16/07	at Oakland	13-14	21-14	20t pass to Anthony Gonzalez	4:49	11-91/5:40	7-7-68, 1 TD pass
9/14/08	at Minnesota	15-15	18-15	Vinatieri 47 FG	0:03	5-21/1:04	1-2-20 pass
		7-15		*32t pass to Reggie Wayne*	*5:54*	*3-61/1:15*	*3-3-61, 1 TD pass*
10/5/08	at Houston	24-27	31-27	5t pass to Reggie Wayne	1:54	2-20/0:42	1-1-5, 1 TD pass
		17-27		*68t Gary Brackett FR*	*3:36*		
		10-27		*7t pass to Tom Santi*	*4:04*	*11-81/4:14*	*8-10-59, 1 TD pass/1-11 rush*
11/2/08	New England	15-15	18-15	Vinatieri 52 FG	8:05	8-48/3:28	2-4-44 pass
11/9/08	at Pittsburgh	17-20	24-20	17t pass to Dominic Rhodes	3:04	4-32/1:40	1-1-17, 1 TD pass

Date	Opponent	Down/Tied	Won	Game-Winning Play	Time Left	Drive/T.O.P.	Manning Drive Stats
11/23/08	at San Diego	20-20	23-20	Vinatieri 51 FG	0:00	8-37/1:30	4-6-36 pass
12/14/08	Detroit	21-21	31-21	1t Rhodes run	8:39	7-88/4:13	4-4-74 pass
9/21/09	at Miami	20-23	27-23	48t pass to Pierre Garcon	3:18	4-80/0:32	3-4-80, 1 TD pass
11/1/09	San Francisco	12-14	18-14	Addai 22t pass to Reggie Wayne	14:53	9-70/3:10	4-6-30 pass
11/8/09	Houston	13-17	20-17	2t Addai run	7:11	8-61/3:49	3-4-38 pass
11/15/09	New England	28-34	35-34	1t pass to Reggie Wayne	0:13	4-29/1:47	2-2-16, 1 TD pass
		21-34		*4t Addai run*	*2:23*	*6-79/1:49*	*4-5-44 pass*
		14-31		*29t pass to Pierre Garcon*	*12:14*	*5-79/2:04*	*3-3-59, 1 TD pass*
11/22/09	at Baltimore	14-15	17-15	Stover 25 FG	7:02	9-60/3:10	4-5-52 pass
11/29/09	at Houston	14-20	35-27	6t pass to Dallas Clark	8:24	7-89/2:50	4-4-49, 1 TD pass
12/17/09	at Jacksonville	28-31	35-31	65t pass to Reggie Wayne	5:23	3-70/0:42	2-3-70, 1 TD pass
10/10/10	Kansas City	9-9	19-9	Vinatieri 42 FG	14:40	12-60/3:46	3-7-23 pass
1/2/11	Tennessee	20-20	23-20	Vinatieri 43 FG	0:00	5-37/1:25	2-3-31 pass
9/9/12	**Pittsburgh**	**19-22**	**31-19**	**1t pass to Jacob Tamme**	**9:23**	**6-80/4:48**	**6-7-57, 1 TD pass**
10/15/12	**at San Diego**	**21-24**	**35-24**	**21t pass to Brandon Stokley**	**9:03**	**3-50/2:08**	**2-2-27, 1 TD pass**
		14-24		*7t pass to Eric Decker*	*13:33*	*9-55/4:14*	*4-4-48, 1 TD pass*
11/4/12	**at Cincinnati**	**17-20**	**31-20**	**1t pass to Joel Dreessen**	**11:47**	**3-46/5:02**	**4-4-50, 1 TD pass**
10/6/13	**at Dallas**	**48-48**	**51-48**	**Prater 28 FG**	**0:02**	**8-14/1:57**	**2-2-21 pass**
		41-48		*1t Moreno run*	*2:39*	*9-73/4:40*	*5-5-77 pass*
		38-41		*Prater 50 FG*	*9:37*	*11-51/4:01*	*5-9-42 pass*
10/27/13	**Washington**	**21-21**	**45-21**	**35t pass to Knowshon Moreno**	**14:19**	**1-35/0:10**	**1-1-35 pass**
		14-21		*1t pass to Joel Dreessen*	*14:56*	*16-83/4:59*	*6-10-67 pass*
11/23/14	**Miami**	**25-28**	**39-36**	**10t C.J. Anderson run**	**5:01**	**11-70/6:16**	**6-7-71 pass**
10/4/15	**Minnesota**	**20-20**	**23-20**	**McManus 39 FG**	**1:41**	**9-55/3:20**	**2-4-28 pass**
10/18/15	**at Cleveland**	**23-23**	**26-23**	**McManus 34 FG**	**4:56 OT**	**13-72/6:42**	**4-4-39 pass**
1/3/16	**vs. San Diego**	**20-20**	**27-20**	**23t Hillman run**	**4:50**	**1-23/0:06**	**0-0-0**

References

Books

Chappell, Mike, with Richards, Phil. *Tales from the Indianapolis Colts Sideline: A Collection of the Greatest Colts Stories Ever Told.* New York: Sports Publishing, 2012

Fischer, David. *The Super Bowl: The First Fifty Years of America's Greatest Game.* New York, Sports Publishing, 2015

Manning, Peyton, Manning, Archie with Underwood, John. *Manning.* New York, HarperCollins, 2001

Mason, Andrew, *Tales from the Denver Broncos Sideline: A Collection of the Greatest Broncos Stories Ever Told.* New York: Sports Publishing, 2014

Myers, Gary. *Brady vs. Manning: The Untold Story of the Rivalry that Transformed the NFL.* New York, Crown, 2015

Periodicals and Websites

Associated Press
bloomberg.com
Dailymail.co.uk
Indianapolis Star
Denver Post
denverbroncos.com
ESPN
Fox News
Knight Ridder Tribune News Service
Los Angeles Times
nfl.com

Newsweek.com
New York Times
The New Yorker
peytonmanning.com/peyback-foundation
Profootballreference.com
profootballtalk.nbcsports.com
Sports Illustrated
sports-reference.com
stampedblue.com
USA Today
YouTube

Image credits

Page 59:	AP Photo/Jack Dempsey	Page 76:	AP Photo/Tom Strickland
Page 60:	AP Photo/Charlie Riedel; AP Photo Charlie Riedel	Page 77:	Courtesy of the Indianapolis Colts
		Page 78:	iStock
Page 61:	Courtesy of the Denver Broncos	Page 80:	Mike Morbeck via Wikimedia Commons; AP Photo
Page 62:	AP Photo/Gregory Payan; Author's Collection		
		Page 84:	AP Photo/David Zalubowski
Page 63:	Courtesy of the Denver Broncos	Page 85:	Courtesy of the Indianapolis Colts
Page 64:	AP Photo/Gregory Payan	Page 92:	Courtesy of the Indianapolis Colts
Page 66:	Courtesy of the Indianapolis Colts	Page 94:	Courtesy of the Indianapolis Colts
Page 67:	Courtesy of the Indianapolis Colts; AP Photo/ Pablo Martinez Monsivais	Page 97:	Courtesy of the Indianapolis Colts
		Page 108:	Courtesy of the Indianapolis Colts; Jeffrey Beall via Wikimedia Commons
Page 68:	AP Photo/David Zalubowski		
Page 70:	iStock	Page 109:	United States Marine Corps/Sgt. D. R. Cotton via Wikimedia Commons; Courtesy of the Indianapolis Colts
Page 72:	Courtesy of PMCH in Indianapolis		
Page 73:	AP Photo/Tom Strickland		
Page 74:	US Navy via Wikimedia Commons	Page 110:	Courtesy of the Indianapolis Colts
Page 75:	U.S. Air Force photo by Master Sgt. Chuck Marsh via Wikimedia Commons